"Successfully launching any freelance business is hard work. Doing it quickly is even more difficult. But, with this engaging, readable, realistic, detailed, practical, and comprehensive roadmap by your side—written by someone who's been there—I really like your chances. Highly recommended."

—Peter Bowerman, Author
The Well-Fed Writer and
The Well-Fed Self-Publisher

"If you're starting out as a freelancer or consultant seeking corporate clients, *Real Skills, Real Income* will help you land business quickly and confidently. With Diana Schneidman's step-by-step guide, you'll avoid expensive, time-wasting mistakes, and begin earning an income sooner than you might have thought possible."

—C.J. Hayden, Author
Get Clients Now!

"This book is like having a really smart, sassy, and caring coach by your side, guiding you to start your freelance writing business and make money. But Diana Schneidman offers great advice for any business. And, really, anyone who has a chapter called 'non-yucky networking' is my kind of business advisor."

—Tama Kieves, Author
*Inspired & Unstoppable: Wildly
Succeeding in Your Life's Work!*

"Diana Schneidman nails what it takes to get your own freelance business up and running. It is truly the solopreneurs's guide to everything that matters! Her practical approach to getting started fast provides comprehensive tools, tips, and techniques. It helps you cut to the chase and offers a blueprint to follow, eliminating time-wasters and maximizing opportunity. This is a must read for everyone thinking of leaving their corporate job to start their own business."

—Gail Zelitzky
Owner, You're in Business...I'm Your Coach!, www.gailzelitzky.com

"This practical book offers support and encouragement for the marketing-averse freelancer. Not only does Schneidman take the reader step by step through the process of finding work; she also debunks common advice that usually offers little payoff. Every new or underemployed freelancer should read this book for a different perspective on how to grow a business and should follow its advice—if only for 30 days, when the inbox is likely to be full."

—Laurie Lewis
Author, *What to Charge: Pricing Strategies for Freelancers and Consultants*

"The purpose-driven millennials I work with are finding it increasingly difficult to land traditional corporate jobs in today's unstable job market. Diana Schneidman's book gives them the tools to reinvent the way they make a living by becoming solopros—expert freelancers and consultants who can master a skill set and get paying clients quickly. The resources she provides, including a checklist of 15 easy actions anyone can do today to get their freelancing business up and running, are invaluable for those looking to succeed in today's economy."

—Adam S. Poswolsky
Author, *The Quarter-Life Breakthrough*

"Have you been laid off, fired or simply need to leave the corporate life for family or health reasons? Diana Schneidman's *Real Skills, Real Income* may be the godsend book you need."

—Joan Friedlander
Author, *Business from Bed: The 6-Step Comeback Plan to Get Yourself Working After a Health Crisis*

"This is an invaluable book at a time when many thousands need it. Job insecurity, ageism, and devastated pension funds mean that mature professionals urgently need practical career alternatives more than ever. Diana Schneidman's book is a uniquely practical resource which will enable you to unlock a future where you don't need a job to survive and thrive. It's a succinct, readable, and proven step-by-step guide for anyone who wants to successfully transition from a corporate paycheck to successful consulting 'solopro' work in just 30 days. Read this book, follow its advice diligently, and you'll never worry about having a job again."

—Neil Patrick
Editor, 40pluscareerguru.blogspot.com

"Just read Diana Schneidman's *Real Skills, Real Income*, and now I can ... breathe! Diana's get-it-done-now advice freed me from the shackles of overthinking. Her list of 'Don't Do's' (my favorite) is a dream come true for those struggling to better manage their time."

—Melzetta "Mele" Williams
Digital Media Writer, www.webtvbymel.com

"You may think you've heard this type of advice before, but you haven't heard it from Diana Schneidman. It's clear that she has battled her own inner wimp and won. She knows the joys and challenges of self-employment, and (as a bonus) she has a wicked sense of humor. When I started reading her book, I found myself laughing out loud and nodding my head at some of her comments. Been there, done that."

—Janet Tilden
Executive Rewrites, www.exec-rewrites.com

"Diana Schneidman helped me jumpstart my freelance career with no-nonsense advice and a valuable stepwise approach. Her book demystified the life of a solo professional and provided me with exactly what I needed to take the leap. When I need new clients, I know exactly what to do. More importantly, I know what NOT to do. I am forever grateful. I love my new career!"

—Sophia Martha Cook
Owner, Larkspur Consulting, LLC, larkspurconsultingllc.com

"What I like most about this book is Diana's unceasing optimism. She does not promise novice solopros a painless journey or instant success. But her practical, down-to-earth advice is easy to follow with just the right boost of insight and wisdom to keep novice, and experienced, solo practitioners moving forward."

—Michele Jiménez
the corporate newswriter, Michele-jimenez.com

"This is your 'get out of corporate jail free' card. It's the only book you'll need to succeed as a freelancer."

—Sandra Beckwith
25+ year freelancer, www.buildbookbuzz.com

"I've been self-employed since 2000, and I've read dozens of business books over the years. This is the most practical book for freelancers that I've ever read. If you're considering doing freelance work, then reading *Real Skills, Real Income* is the ideal place to start. Don't wait. Buy this book now and benefit from Diana Schneidman's wisdom."

—Stephen H. Lahey
Host, SmallBusinessTalent.com

"Diana's book is a must read for professionals. It teaches the basics of the real life skills needed to 'make it' in the working world. *Real Skills, Real Income* discusses the important communication skills and the necessity to draft a realistic plan for your career."

—Shalom Klein
Chairman, Jewish B2B Networking, Publisher,
Jewish Business News

"Wish I knew the magic words to make Diana Schneidman's *Real Skills, Real Income* stand out on a crowded shelf as admirably as its content stands out from the crowd of freelancing how-to's. With humor and clarity, *Real Skills, Real Income* teaches readers to work solo."

—Judith West
Audiobook narrator, producer, coach, www.judithwest.com

Real Skills, Real Income

A Proven Marketing System to Land Well-Paid Freelance and Consulting Work in 30 Days or Less

DIANA SCHNEIDMAN

First Edition

Stand Up 8 Times
www.StandUp8Times.com

Chicago • Bolingbrook

Stand Up 8 Times
PO Box 932
Bolingbrook, IL 60440

Publisher's Cataloging-In-Publication Data
(Prepared by The Donohue Group, Inc.)

Schneidman, Diana.
   Real skills, real income : a proven marketing system to land well-paid freelance and consulting work in 30 days or less / by Diana Schneidman. -- 1st ed.

   p. ; cm.

   Includes index.
   Issued also as an ebook.
   ISBN: 978-0-9910153-0-6

   1. Marketing. 2. Consulting firms--Marketing. 3. Self-employed--Marketing.
4. Success in business. I. Title.

HF5415 .S36 2014
658.85   2013952941

18 17 16 15 14   10 9 8 7 6 5 4 3 2 1

To Faye, Herschel, and Eli, who inspired and witnessed my freelance and consulting experiments.

To Wayne, my sounding board, husband, and best friend through years of career meanderings and growth, including the writing of this book.

Disclaimer

The information presented herein represents the views of the author as of the date of publication. Because of the rate at which conditions change, the author reserves the right to alter and update her opinions based on new conditions.

The book is for informational purposes only. While every attempt has been made to verify the information provided in this book, neither the author nor her affiliates and partners assume any responsibility for errors, inaccuracies, or omissions. Any reference to any person or business whether living or dead is coincidental. Any slights of people or organizations are unintentional.

If advice concerning legal or related matters is needed, the services of a fully qualified professional should be sought. This book is not intended for use as a source of legal or accounting advice. You should be aware of any laws which govern business transactions or other business practices in your country and state and other appropriate jurisdictions.

Every effort has been made to represent the book and its potential accurately. Please remember that each individual's success depends on his/her background, dedication, desire, motivation, and other circumstances. As with any business endeavor, there is no guarantee that you will earn any money. Always perform full due diligence and seek appropriate professional advice when contemplating any business endeavor or investment opportunity.

Please do not construe any statement in this document as a claim or representation of average earnings. There are no average earnings. Testimonials and statements of individuals are not to be construed as claims or representations of average earnings. The author makes no claims as to earnings, average or otherwise.

Upon purchase of this book, you are granted permission to use this document solely for your own personal use and not for republication, distribution, assignment, sublicense, sale, preparation of derivative works, or other use.

Table of Contents

What to say when they ask, "Why you?"

Calculating the odds. (They're a lot better than Vegas.)

Why rejection is amazingly rare.

The three top ways to bill.

If you compete on price, you'll hope not to win.

What to say when a prospect asks your rates.

Charge what you're worth. (So, what are you worth?)

Why low start-out rates don't lock you into a lifetime of undercharging.

Should you negotiate your rates?

How much to bill your mother.

Inventory control when your time is for sale.

How to collect $ quickly.

If you don't manage yourself, no one else will do it for you.

Full-time work is fewer hours than you think.

Tomorrow is a new day, not today's catch up day.

How (and whether) to solopro when you have a full-time job.

Establish your own business in 15 fast actions.

How to build out each initial action over time.

17 widely recommended marketing tools to take off your to-do list (ah, that feels so good).

Author note: The chapter subheads in the preceding table of contents do not correlate to actual subheads in the book. This was done intentionally to help you, prior to purchase, quickly grasp the subjects covered. The chapter titles and the index at the end of the book will help you find the information you seek.

Introduction

My story . . .

I'll never forget the day I came home from work and prepared to give my three children the bad news.

My eyes were red from sobbing in the car, but I tried to pull myself together as I stacked up cardboard boxes of framed photos and used pens by my home desk.

"I have something to tell you," I started, struggling to hold back the tears.

"You've been fired again, right?"

Leave it to a kid to cut right to the chase.

Yes, it was true.

It was "again" that really stung.

You see, despite my proven marketing and writing skills, employment troubles followed me like my shadow.

This was the fourth time I'd been kicked out of payroll jobs.

First it was after disability leave expired (I'm fine now, thank God), but the next two times were female problems—in other words, office politics between other women and myself.

The fourth time I refused to commit unethical practices and they dumped me the following Friday. (They didn't explain why, but I could guess.)

So here I was again. Unemployed and short on funds.

This time I made my decision in an instant: I would immediately re-start my home business as a freelancer and consultant while looking for another payroll job.

However, I had a serious problem: While I had clients in the past, I lost almost all of them each time I accepted a full-time job.

I make no apologies for letting freelance fall by the wayside. I devoted myself to each corporate job, even taking extra work home. Plus I raised three children on my own and tried to have a life.

But here I was back at square one . . . again. Almost no clients, and leads as cold as stainless steel in December.

The fourth time was the charm. Fortunately, I needed to make money quickly, and by this time the school of hard knocks had taught me the best way to start over. I quickly got my first paying assignments and soon had something—or *several somethings*—on my plate at all times. This book explains exactly what I did and how you can succeed just as I did.

How about you?

Are you unemployed? Underemployed? Or you have a portfolio from college and internship assignments but you haven't pinned down your first real paying job in your field? Perhaps you are in your forties or fifties or even 60-plus and suspect you have experienced age discrimination?

Are you discouraged and frustrated with your job hunt? Uncertain where you're headed and what to do next?

Perhaps you've been in this sad state for a while or maybe you were let go just yesterday. Either way, you may be tempted to sit back and lick your wounds until a solution presents itself. If you have substantial savings and are eligible for unemployment compensation, this may be possible.

But unstructured time can be financially and emotionally costly. Your savings dwindle away while the severance/unemployment benefits clock keeps ticking down . . . or runs out. Plus if you're anything like me, you sink into a funk that keeps coming 'round no matter how many times your companions and motivational audios try to shame you out of self-defeating thought patterns.

Your situation is challenging, but there is an answer: **Start your own business today as a freelancer or consultant, that is, a solo professional—a solopro!**

This answer may overwhelm you with more questions and doubts: *Should I devote myself full-time to a solo practice? Or, should I look for another corporate job at the same time? What is the best path for me?*

If you have been reading and hearing "experts" in the media describe the superhuman motivation and confidence that self-employment requires, yet another question torments you: *Do I have the passion that self-employment requires?*

Here's the short answer to the "passion" dilemma you face if you read the same books as I do:

You don't need passion right now. You don't need the answer to every question and comfort for every self-doubt to get paying work. And, you can start your solo practice and continue with your job search at the same time.

Reaching out to others with your professional services and undertaking assignments will reveal your answers over time. And while passion is terrific—if you have found your passion, more power to you!—your achievements as you build a practice just may boost your spirits and help you recognize the passion (or at least an acceptable career interest) that was invisible amid clouds of gloom.

Perhaps you've been calling yourself a freelancer or consultant for a while now, but you have had no, or few, clients. This book will help you get paying assignments quickly and answer questions that may haunt you—or even paralyze you from taking action.

There are many ways to find freelance or consulting assignments. Intelligent effort, applied consistently over time, will bring you success!

It's easy! But in a hard sort of way.

It's not brain surgery, but simply extracting a splinter from your finger can take a full episode of *Law and Order* and be painful as all get out.

You can do it . . . and by "it," I mean freelancing and consulting. In the coming pages, I'll "put the verbs in my sentences," as daytime TV's Dr. Phil says when he spells out action recommendations to people who are at a loss as to how to solve their problems.

So let's hide the remote under the couch cushion and get to work.

Turn on the money spigot ASAP.

My approach helps you put in place the basic tools you need to start marketing yourself and your services immediately. Yes, right now, as soon as you finish reading this book. Unless friends or ex-employers have already given you assignments, you won't make money until you start marketing. It's not going to happen any other way.

Though you can, and should, start pronto, note that a solo-pro practice takes a while to earn the money you want. There are too many individual variables—your skill level, marketing efforts, social connections, the economy, the local market-place, your specialty—to predict accurately how long it will take to meet your personal financial objectives.

Many highly qualified people need a few weeks of intense prospecting to get their first assignment, and it may take yet more time before they receive an agreement and a deposit check and can start work. It may take much longer to earn top rates consistently.

Face it. That's the nature of the beast. However, generally speaking, many people land their first paying clients within thirty days of reaching out to targeted prospects.

The advice in this book worked for me.

This book developed from my own experiences. I started as a freelance business copywriter in 1992. The only technology I owned was a simple PC with WordPerfect. I had no printer and no Internet access, which was okay since the Internet wasn't on most people's radar yet.

So I resorted to picking up the phone as the best way to generate work quickly.

It took me days to get up enough courage to make my first call, and after each call, I'd have to take a break to calm down and regain my courage to proceed.

When those calls led to leads, I'd head over to the photo-copying shop where I'd spend a fortune on portfolio samples that I would then mail out with a customized cover letter. Each lead required a considerable investment of money *and* time.

Then I'd trudge home six miles in the snow, unharness the

horse, put on my apron, and bring in wood to heat up a cup of coffee.

OK, it was not *that* long ago, but times were somewhat different from today. There were a few books about freelancing and consulting, but not many. I made do with what I could find and improvised as I went.

As the months and years rolled by, phoning became ever easier. After all, the phone is our friend. Everyone has one (or two). It's a lot easier to talk than to write. We are not restricted by how quickly our thumbs tire (if you're into texting) or by 140-character limits (as on Twitter). We've been using the phone all our lives to talk grandma into buying us the toy we want and to charm potential dates into seeing the movies we want to see. Phoning is free (depending on your pricing plan). And as a bonus, it is no longer attached to the wall by a long cord.

Every workday I'd start with my planned number of calls, proud of a measurable achievement first thing in the A.M. I became so relaxed and confident with phoning that I'd make a few more calls to postpone the hard work of writing. There's nothing so great as procrastination that brings in cash. And when I feared the future and its economic uncertainties, I easily convinced myself that I would be able to generate funds come what may.

So can you. *If I can do it, anyone can do it.*

Getting started today can be much easier and cheaper now that the Internet speeds communication and anyone you may work with is online. But with greater access to information comes more conflicting advice. If you are like me, you are deluged with emails chockfull of marketing ideas. Many start out with dire warnings: follow the secret the writer is about to reveal or you will fail miserably. Then they prescribe a huge work list that leaves you gasping for air.

You can't do everything all at once. Even if you are in business for years, there will be many marketing ideas you never test. Your business is a work in progress. *And it always will be.* So you can't—and there's no need to—perfect all your marketing messages, materials, and channels before you go out and get some clients.

If the Internet is feeding you the same stuff it feeds me, it's telling you all day long that people much dumber than us have "cracked the code" and "pulled back the curtain" to easy riches. Other "experts" boast they are realistic—we can hope to make only a few hundred bucks a day with no effort. (As if!)

Hold on a minute, you're thinking. It sounds like this book recommends hard work. Yes, it does prescribe consistent, put-your-back-into-it work. This work requires intense butt-in-chair, time-consuming effort. It demands tuned-in, customer-responsive conversation, not simply rote answers to expected questions. It's not about unearned miracles. This book describes a system that enables adults to succeed in the real world.

It's not easy, but it's not hard either. We regular folks can get down to work and apply what we already have achieved to bring in real income now.

No written business plan in spiral binding? No driving passion? No inspired vision of where you'll be in five years or next month?

So what. It doesn't matter. Let's begin.

A true story about evolution and focus

I belong to a local organization of freelance writers that meets monthly. Many of us go out for dinner after the meeting. A few years ago, a member of the program committee sat at the dinner table and described with both admiration and envy the amazing websites of certain of our peers. One in particular stood out as a comprehensive and mouth-watering display of writing talent.

So a few months later when members of the organization requested a meeting on the subject of how to develop a professional website, it was no surprise that the program committee member invited this website star to speak.

We were eager to hear how the guest speaker developed such a knock-your-socks-off site, but it was clear she saw her accomplishments quite differently. Her current website was less than cutting edge, and she focused on all its shortcomings. Sure, she had posted lots of published articles in leading newspapers and journals as well as marketing pieces for leading corporations. Yes, she had testimonials from prestigious clients. And as proof of the pudding, she was busy with paying assignments.

But she was looking to her next redesign, one that would capture email addresses for her mailing list, optimize better on Google, provide more metrics for evaluating her site, be easier for her to update on the fly, and include a sticky blog. (Remember, this was several years ago.)

That's how it is for every solopro. We're always planning ahead and our vision outpaces reality.

There are two reasons for this. First, as we win clients and perform our services, we both continue to find new opportunities beyond our original specialty and to narrow our niche more effectively. These two forces can be in opposition to each other as we reconsider our direction over time. Both expanding and narrowing will beckon to us throughout our years of practice; we will never finalize our business definition.

Second, technology continues to develop and present new ways to run our business. Years ago it was about creating a website as a brochure. Later, blogging, free email newsletters, and online social networking gained in popularity. That doesn't mean all these choices are right for you, but they will change how you look at your marketing program.

I wrote this book to help you *focus.* The last thing I want is for you to be overwhelmed or lured off course. I wrote this as much to take activities *off* your to-do list as to recommend what you *should* do.

You can't do it all. In fact, it's best to concentrate on only one or two marketing techniques at a time, especially at the beginning. Focus on activities that will bring you gigs and money quickly. The coaching industry labels alluring but optional marketing diversions as Bright Shiny Objects, and these BSOs number in the hundreds or even thousands. (There's more about this later in the book.)

You too can begin imperfectly!

E-business has evolved to the point where you can put the pieces in place, easily and inexpensively, all by yourself. You can revise and improve anything as often as you want, even daily.

Here's a new motto for your new endeavor: *Anything worth doing is worth starting imperfectly.*

To the point:

- Floundering in employment or unemployment woes? Try freelancing and consulting to improve your morale and make some money.

- Work smart. Limit your marketing to one channel (or two) that can bring results quickly.

- Pick up the phone and make some calls. Keep reading and I'll tell you what to say.

Why Go Solopro?

There are a zillion good reasons to set up shop as a consultant or freelancer. Here are some of my favorites:

1. Earn money.

Well, duh. Everyone works to make money, right?

Sure, but this is more of a driver for some people than others. Some people really are content to pursue their interests—or *passion*—and wouldn't mind earning a few bucks for their trouble. That's totally valid and so is going for the gold . . . or at least the silver.

If income is your primary goal, recognize happily (!) that freelancing and consulting tend to pay substantially more per hour than corporate employment.

Taking low-paying assignments at the beginning may be acceptable as you get your feet wet, create a portfolio, assemble references and testimonials, learn from your peers and clients, and simply build up the courage to ask for more money. However, over time you will want to identify and go after the services, industries, and customers that pay well.

Do note a financial downside to freelancing and consulting. While ongoing, effective marketing and customer satisfaction will help generate a more dependable income, self-employment is rarely as consistent as a corporate paycheck. (On the other hand, a full-time employer can terminate you without warning and there you are with all your eggs in a single broken basket.)

2. Create immediate employment.

By dinner tonight, you can honestly say you are employed. Yes, tonight. The day you're reading this book. Start outlining your marketing program, or phone a contact or two, and you're in business! Yeah, it's not your ultimate business, but I already told you that your ultimate business never happens. Taking a step, any step, is your imperfect start.

This doesn't mean you will have any clients by 5 P.M. Nor any income just yet.

Marketing is intrinsic to consulting and freelancing. Marketing in itself is real work for better (yes, you are immediately employed) or worse (it does take effort that will likely not pay off immediately).

3. Establish a continuous work history and eliminate periods of unemployment.

If you continue to look for a corporate job, you need a traditional résumé. And a résumé is reviewed with suspicion if it doesn't clearly present an uninterrupted work history.

Forming your own solopro practice fills in the current employment gap to demonstrate career continuity. Instead of listing a variety of temp assignments, freelance gigs, part-time jobs, and volunteer activities as separate jobs, give them a single heading. Then bullet your achievements underneath that.

4. Learn and demonstrate new skills in the real world. Explore and expand career interests.

It's incredible but true: People will pay you to do things as an independent that they would never find you qualified to do as an employee.

This, alas, flips common sense on its head. The large company has executives, supervisors, and coworkers, assembled in scads of meetings and extensive review chains, to train and oversee workers. Whenever you have a question, there's someone nearby to ask. You also have access to professional subscriptions, seminars, expensive equipment, and lots of other stuff paid for by someone else.

Yet corporate job postings tend to be highly rigid and demanding, requesting individuals with five years of experience doing the exact same work as will be done in the position being filled.

On the other hand, the prospects you phone will propose solopro opportunities substantially different from anything you have ever done in the past. You will be presented with assignments for which your qualifications are moderate, even questionable.

You'll offer your services to design thingamabobs, and they'll ask if you can sell thingamajigs. Even if you are honest and say, "Thingamabob design is my greater strength, but I'd be interested in working under your guidance on the thingamajig," they may well give you the opportunity.

Or you can identify in advance an area into which you would like to expand. I've tried spin-off specialties by detailing how my qualifications in one area relate to my new target assignment.

It could be that the most important characteristic of corporate employers is a fear of commitment. They'd rather allow freelancers and consultants to try new specialties than hire full-timers for the same type of career switch. Even though a temp assignment may last for months, it doesn't last forever. Their decision isn't irrevocable. (As if they aren't ready to dump loyal employees in a heartbeat! But you know what I mean.)

5. Escape corporate stress.

Many years ago Johnny Paycheck sang, "Take this job and shove it."

We've long recognized the pleasures of self-employment: wear what you want, do what you want, sleep when you want, amuse yourself when you want, and ideally, have enough money for all these pursuits and more. But lately there is an even more compelling justification for self-employment: the more widespread, and more extreme, dysfunction of many corporate workplaces.

The stress is huge these days, in case you haven't noticed. Corporate employees are falling apart from the craziness. Office insanity is the underlying cause of silly arguments, temperamental blow-ups, withholding of critical info, and most important, conflicting and impossible demands on staff.

Now I don't have numbers to support my theory—I can't even suggest ways the Departments of Commerce or Labor would measure it—but the anecdotal evidence is pretty convincing. The atmosphere in the modern office is highly toxic. Psychological cyanide is billowing out the A/C vents and saturating those long beige hallways and gray cubicles. What a time and energy drain the typical office has become!

Becoming a solopro frees you from omnipresent corporate stress. The best thing about freelancing is that you can limit your exposure to tension to ten-minute blocks of time, all of them on the phone. You commiserate when the client is pressured or fearful, try to offer useful input into their work in progress, and convince them you know what you're doing and the results will be fine.

Then you hang up, go about your work, and thank God you don't sit in their office. Or you sit back with your coffee or turn on Dr. Phil or go for a walk. But mostly you smile, knowing it is their problem, not yours.

Or perhaps it is your problem. Their stress is becoming your stress.

There's a solution for this too. As a solopro, you are always looking for the next assignment. Simply redouble your efforts to get better clients.

6. Be treated like a valued professional.

Generally speaking, your consulting and freelance clients value your expertise much more than your corporate supervisors did. I think there are two reasons for this. First, clients know only your credentials and your output. They haven't witnessed your weaknesses—your tendency to nod off during hours-long meetings or how you rely on a calculator for the simplest arithmetic functions or your Starbucks addiction—and have nary a clue to your personal insecurities. No familiarity, no contempt.

Second, the people who hire you to solopro wholeheartedly want you to succeed. Since you're out of sight, you present no political risk to them. Everything you do well makes the person who brought you in for the project look good, and no matter how impressive your work, your corporate liaison has no fear that you—someone who may be completely unknown to the rest of the organization—can threaten his spot on the corporate pyramid.

7. Write your own employee manual.

Maybe this should be moved to the top of the list. There are so many advantages to self-employment (when you're working at home) if you allow them.

Some experts recommend that although you work at home, you should dress up as if you're going to the most conservative office in the world—complete with necktie or high heels. It's a trick, they say, that creates a certain vibe that then enables you to achieve professional quality even though you are seated in your bedroom in front of your computer.

If dressing professionally were necessary to deliver professional-level work, my career would be in shambles. I love to dress in sweatsuits or shorts and it doesn't impede my productivity in any way.

That's the point of self-employment. You can dress, schedule your time, play music, and eat snacks however, wherever, and whenever you choose. All that matters is that the work gets done as expected, that you market consistently, and that you present a professional image to the client (an image that may be conveyed solely by phone and email in many cases).

If you are conscientious and self-disciplined, having flexibility in your scheduling and lifestyle is heavenly. Don't you forget it.

8. Improve your negotiating position for a full-time job.

When you are idle and steadily spending down your assets, you may jump at any job offer, no matter how unappealing or underpaid. When you have some solopro work on your plate, you quiet the desperation and can present your case more assertively. Now you have success stories from your solopro experience that add breadth and substance to your portfolio (if relevant to your job objectives). And while comparing salaries to solopro hourly rates is not apples to apples, you can document your current value in the marketplace.

9. Tend to your children and other family (and life) obligations.

Many offices have no sympathy for situations that arise outside the office, transforming typical home glitches into job-threatening catastrophes. The boss has the power to forbid you from waiting for the furnace repair guy to show up or dropping off a misplaced field-trip permission slip at the school. Despite staying late as needed and meeting all deadlines, I dreaded bringing these situations to my supervisors' attention.

There are so many events that don't merit excused absence in the employee manual but are important to us. Funerals of community acquaintances and friends' parents, visits from out-of-towners, standing in line to buy Tickle Me Elmo, driving Mom to the podiatrist, and perfect weather at the pool.

Soloproing relieves great chunks of the stress in my life. I handle what needs to be handled when it needs to be handled and answer to no one but myself. When my children were young, I'd tell callers that I was on my way out to a meeting. Actually, I was rushing them to the doctor to get scrips for recurring ear infections. (In my corporate days, I'd totally freak out when my child would wake up at 3 A.M. with an earache.)

It's important to present a professional image to the client regardless of what is really going on at home. My children knew that when I was on the phone with a *customer*—a label I used for everyone from a client to an information source—they were not to disturb me.

Freelancing or consulting does not extend the number of hours in the day. The math just doesn't permit all that a full-time parent does and all that a full-time worker does simultaneously. If you have young children, you may well need day-care or other paid assistance to manage a full work schedule. But solopro self-employment does give you the flexibility to determine how you will creatively schedule those twenty-four hours. That's sure better than working in someone else's office and having to ask permission to take care of what needs to be done at home.

I could warn you not to let housework encroach on your work time but I won't. I regularly toss in a load of laundry before I sit down at my desk. It's called multitasking. Executives are so proud of their ability to answer emails and take phone calls at the same time they fire people. Multitasking works for me too.

10. Avoid discrimination due to age, pregnancy, weight, disability, race, or any other factors.

What seems to be a big deal if you've been turned down for numerous full-time jobs generally fades to irrelevance when you present yourself as a freelancer or consultant. Nobody cares.

For starters, it may be that no one knows. Since you may never see clients face to face, they often won't know this kind of personal detail unless you tell them. And why would you?

Second, what seems to matter a great deal when they are hiring a payroll worker doesn't matter for the short term. In part this may be because you will not receive health insurance (for U.S. readers). Or it may be that your long-term outlook doesn't matter. The only question is whether you can physically handle the current assignment in the designated timeframe.

Third, a consulting or freelance relationship is much less intense. Rapport factors that supposedly mean a whole

bunch within a corporate environment don't enter into remote, telephone- or e-mail-centered relationships. Sadly,
corporate requirements for rapport and corporate culture are
often euphemisms for demographic compatibility. The young
guys tossing Nerf balls and downing beers need other young
guys to toss balls and drink beer with. (Did you see *The Social
Network*, the movie about Facebook's origins?)

A bit (or a lot) of paunch, gray hair, remembering the Bea-
tles (or even Elvis) on *Ed Sullivan*—none of these hinder the
launch of a freelance or consulting practice as they do when
trolling for a corporate job.

11. Repair your soul.

Have you been beaten down by an oppressive work environment in which you were terminated—or pushed to resign—
by hostile management, catty coworkers, corporate politics,
project failures, or budget shortfalls?

Then, have you faced discouragement and intense competition while seeking full-time employment? When you discuss the job market with others, are you told that it's you who
are projecting the wrong message to the universe in your de-
pressed mental state? That you exude, and therefore attract,
negativity? In other words, *that you are your problem*?

You need a positive response from the universe to break the
cycle. Soloproing can repair your soul, nourish your outlook.

As you call around for assignments, positive feedback
awaits you. True, these quick pats on the back and positive
feedback will not be consistent. On the other hand, outright
rejection is surprisingly rare, especially if you wisely refrain
from labeling no response—the most common response to
your marketing—as rejection. *Most people don't care enough to
reject you*!

You will learn profoundly that "no" is a fact of life and not to take it personally. You will work your way out of being overly sensitive. And the prize is worth it. You can get assignments that remind you of better days and restore your self-confidence. These successes can be as valuable as cash.

12. It's fun.

After working at a corporate job, freelancing or consulting is a lot more fun. You're the captain of the ship, you determine the route. You are in charge. You can adjust your schedule, work style, manner of clothing, and habits to your own pleasure. No more griping at the water cooler since this is what you have chosen for yourself.

13. It's your dream.

Perhaps you've been yearning for self-employment for years. If this is your reason, 'nuff said (for now).

To the point:

- There are so many good reasons to try the solopro life. Reason number one is to earn some money.

- Declare yourself a solopro and you're employed this very moment—although it may take a little time to bring in some money.

- Escape office stress as a solopro and improve your work life.

- Be your own boss. Create your own work rules. Integrate your work with your life. Love your life.

Step 1

Jump-Start Your Business:
Three Guiding Ideas

How can I jump-start my solopro practice?

As I look back on my own experience as a solopro, beginning in 1992, and research how others succeed in similar quests, I propose three guiding ideas:

First, offer a service as similar as possible to what you did in your last good full-time job. You'll have the most self-confidence when you offer the work you know best. Plus you will have the qualifications—years of experience, success stories and war stories, a portfolio, college degrees, certificates and credentials, association memberships, etc.—that will easily convince prospects that you've got the talent for the assignment.

Remember that solopros must be able to work independently. The stronger your background in specific duties, skills, and industries, the easier it will be to produce client-pleasing work that meets tight deadlines from the relative isolation of a home office.

The alternative to my advice? Well, many advisors recommend that when you are at these transitional crossroads, you should determine your passion and pursue it wholeheartedly.

Sounds good, but in practice, it's easiest to get paying assignments quickly by aligning your efforts with your qualifications.

Don't let that passion thing distort your judgment.

I remember the first time I heard that if your work is like play, you will never have to work another day in your life. That sounded good to me! It inspired me, in fact, to spend years second guessing every work decision with one question: *Is this really my passion?*

I realized over time that passion—at least for me—is a moving target. I have that strong passion when pursuing a new idea, a new project. I'm riding high. Then I face a tedious or difficult problem that saps my enthusiasm. It may be that I need a specific fact I can't track down or that I have lots of boring data to input. Then my passion seeps away and I determine that the project must not be in the realm of my passion. Then I work through the problem and finish on a high note, proud that I've accomplished my goal and that the client is pleased. Then once again I feel passion and I'm motivated. Hmm.

Over time I discovered that all projects involving research and writing, my primary strengths, followed a V form. High start, descending to the pit, and concluding on another high.

Eventually I scratched passion as a determinant for what I should do. All work followed the same trajectory, so I chose the niche with the greatest profit potential. And I recognized I must stick with a project even when it turns ugly, confident that I can work through the problem and triumph, in a burst of passion, at the end.

Second, contact the best prospects individually. Your best prospects are employed at full-time corporate jobs and work under a great deal of pressure. Though self-employed individuals may find time to explore Facebook, Twitter, networking events, etc., the people most likely to buy your work are engulfed in on-the-job firefighting. They are too busy to note your existence unless you reach out and tap them directly on the figurative shoulder.

Third, get real! Let's define quickly as thirty days, not thirty minutes. Much as you would like to start making money with your first phone call, this rarely happens. It may require a substantial number of phone calls, but with planning and discipline these initial calls can be completed in a month or less. Though there may seem to be minimal response to your first calls, as the days pass, you'll begin to see results. And since as a solo practitioner you can only handle a limited number of assignments simultaneously, your schedule may fill up quickly.

Most other prospecting techniques require much more time to kick in. Networking and online social networking (e.g., Facebook, Twitter, LinkedIn) require prospects to know, like, and trust you. Such relationships obviously require nurturing over time. Website development, search engine optimization, and other sophisticated practices also may require several months or longer to fill your practice.

Is phoning always the right path for every individual? Of course not. Making a living, or mapping your life's journey, is a unique process for each of us. Our education and experience, skills and preferences, personalities and attitudes, perhaps even our missions and destinies, lead us to choose how we will manage our work campaigns in ways that are singularly right for us.

While the three guiding ideals above are not ideal for everyone—and conflict with much of the advice out there in the marketplace—they may well be just right for you! If you're not convinced at this point, keep an open mind and read on. Simply sleep on it. That's not so difficult, is it?

Wait a minute . . . Do I really have to phone people?

The choice is yours.

Of course you don't *have to*. Plenty of people have built successful practices differently.

But if you offer a product or service that helps others, why wouldn't you want to share the good news as directly as possible with the people most likely to benefit from what you offer?

The good news is that telephoning is easier than most people think it is. It's not about aggressive *selling*. It's not about saying the magic word to transform customers into helpless purchasing zombies under your magnetic selling spell. It's not about persistence as though if at first they say no, you can convert them into buyers against their will by bludgeoning them with more pressure.

It's not about pestering people. It's about helping them. *Really*. You are simply helping people by calling those most likely to benefit from your services. You briefly explain what you do to see if they may want your services. You write down notes so you can follow up on a reasonable schedule. Then on to the next call.

This *is* easy once you learn how to do it and get past the first few calls. Clear the initial hurdle and you can do this! The work of identifying and phoning prospects is a bit repetitive and isn't necessarily what we would choose to do for all that time if we didn't want to succeed. But, this is a system that works, and a system that works is the happiest, most pleasant, most rewarding way to build your business . . . by far!

So reach out and phone people. Phoning takes less time to gear up because it doesn't have to be word perfect. Your script—or mere outline—isn't available to prospects for their close scrutiny so you can polish and personalize your message as you go. There's a higher probability that your contacts will be aware you called than with most other methods of contact, and depending on your phone plan, the call is probably free. Phoning requires minimal preparation and targets the individuals and companies that most need your services. (Keep reading and I'll tell you what to say.)

Plus it replaces a daily goal you can't control—how much business you land each day—with something entirely in your control—how many dials you make each day. You set your target number and when you're done, that's it. You feel wonderful, having completed a day's work. You are not emotionally dependent on the "thumbs up" of others to determine if you've had a good day or a bad day. Every day you meet your call projections, not your sales projections, is a successful day.

Furthermore, when you have a single marketing action planned for the day, all other marketing activities fall to the wayside. You eliminate distractions and conflicting demands upon your time. Your to-do list is nice and short; you can complete it!

What is the most important attitude to adopt?

Self-confidence! And self-knowledge of your abilities.

Your most important personal belief is that your work and your service are exceptional. You care deeply about your clients and do the best you can for them. You deserve top rates.

Are these your beliefs? If not, make them true or get out of the business. Are you exceptional? Then believe you will succeed. And if you don't believe you are exceptional? Why not?

If this is something you can fix, *fix it immediately*. Need more training? *Sign up for it*. Spend money on it if necessary. (Note that learning is a lifelong pursuit for professionals. I'm talking about what you need to learn right now to get started.)

Need more experience? *Get it.* It may be worth your while to work for free or at a low rate for a volunteer organization or smaller company. If you feel comfortable with the arrangement and are learning, you are not being taken advantage of.

Perhaps modesty is your downfall. This is a real problem. Believe in yourself and *live* this belief. This doesn't mean being a loud mouth or altering your personality, but it does mean expanding your comfort zone and finding the way to make these calls that works for you. And, hey, maybe the old you wouldn't have made such calls, but the new you is a self-employed solopro!

The right people want to hear from you, even if they don't know it yet.

When you believe in your services, it is apparent that phoning well-chosen prospects is not being a pest. Thoughtful emails are not spam. You are helping people by letting them know your assistance is available. *You are helping them solve problems.*

The right people are glad to have found you. Some prospects will engage you in long conversations, and some will return your phone messages promptly. Some will save your name for a project down the road or pass it to a coworker, and you may never know that this has happened until months or even years in the future.

Sometimes you hit upon the right person at the right moment. This synchronization of the universe is called *serendipity* or *God winks.* For instance, I recently happened to phone an insurance agent who had written an article he wanted to submit to an insurance publication but he didn't know how to transform the piece from a transcription of his thoughts to a well-organized article ready for publication. He was ready to talk and a check soon followed.

With every call, you are helping another individual and his

or her company, right? Doesn't this thought motivate you to help more people every day? And of course, to earn the money you deserve for giving this assistance?

How can I know in advance if I will succeed as a solopro?

I worked with a new coaching client who asked this very question before embarking on a telephone campaign for freelance assignments. A good question. A natural question. One we all ask when starting out.

Of course there are no guarantees in life.

But here are some answers.

It worked for me. On several occasions I found myself in touchy financial situations after termination from full-time jobs. I needed some freelance work and, by golly, I restarted the cash flow quickly by applying my three guiding ideas.

An effective system, implemented with intensity, works! Now I'm not saying I was rolling in money—or even work—in no time flat. Just as perfecting your tennis serve, learning a new job, or building a bookcase all require persistent effort, so does marketing.

Determined and consistent effort pays off. Spotty effort doesn't. This is delving into a finer point of what I state above. If you don't put forth much effort to get assignments, you probably won't get much work. Magic happens but it's slower than abracadabra. More like abra-cadabra-cadabra and sometimes not till the rabbit is settled in his cage for the night.

Success rarely happens overnight. Allow thirty days and see for yourself. Not very long in real life, but it feels like thirty years in Internet time and even longer to a toddler waiting till after dinner for a cookie.

You may strike gold on day one. It's happened to me. I've

made my first few calls after an extended spell making no calls at all and then I get an out-of-the-blue call from a client of years past.

Too much assessment, handwringing, and navel gazing wastes phoning time and is counterproductive. Questioning the process after every call is akin to the dieter who weighs herself every time she goes to the bathroom. Misleading and discouraging. Don't kid yourself—this isn't useful analysis. It's fuel for doubt and procrastination. Quit thinking and put judgment aside. The vast majority of calls will not yield work—and certainly not immediate assignments. *It's the process as a whole that is effective!*

Finally, here is what I most know:

If you don't try it, it certainly won't work! Proactive, consistent marketing pays off. Inaction does not!

To the point:

- Offer a service similar to your last good job.

- Proactive phoning is the most direct method of contacting those who need your help.

- The people you can best help want to hear from you. You have something of real value to offer them.

- Get real. Give yourself thirty days of consistent effort to achieve results.

- Apply dedicated, consistent effort over time and you will achieve the results you desire.

Step 2

Determine Your Service and Your Niche

To start landing assignments, we've got to decide what types of assignments we are going after. This entire book is about how to take action early and adjust what we are doing as we go. Realistically speaking, this adjustment process will continue till the day we flat-out totally retire. No matter how well thought out it may be, one decision can't be expected to be so perfect that it withstands our changing interests, marketplace trends, economic ups and downs, and the myriad other factors that compel further thought and change.

So don't give in to analysis paralysis. Choose a starter direction and get going. For most of us, the best place to start is with work we already know. In other words, let's look at our last good job and extract a skill at which we've already proven ourselves and can apply in a solopro format.

How to select a niche?

First, what's a niche? Technically speaking, *niche* is defined as the service you provide, as opposed to *target market*, the group of people (or companies) served. The niche may be writing or computer programming or designing sewage systems. The target market describes your audience, such as small-business owners or podiatrist offices or urban sewage departments (whatever they happen to be formally called). You'll need to determine both your niche and your target market.

Many of the so-called experts recommend starting a business by selecting your niche. Grab a blank sheet of paper and a pencil, sit down at the kitchen table, and get to work. *Let's get it done this afternoon so we can start marketing, right?*

Uh, sorry, it doesn't work like that in real life. We can make an initial, broad pass at this determination so we *can* start marketing immediately. But the refined niche that we want long-term finds us more slowly as we test our positioning within the marketplace.

If you want to start earning money quickly as a freelancer or consultant, choose an initial niche similar to your last good job. This makes life easier during start-up.

How to refine a niche

A niche can be refined—or even changed—over time. This does not mean that we made the wrong choice the first time or that we have trouble sticking with something. Some of the most inspired and dedicated individuals change their niches several times during their careers as they learn new things about themselves or identify new needs in the marketplace.

Take new media titans Facebook and Twitter. They couldn't have adopted this niche more than a few years ago because social media didn't exist. Consider the many graphic designers who made the leap from print work to website design as the former dried up and clients requested more of the latter.

Others adapt their niches to different industries, specific branches of the same industry, or certain target audiences identified either by demographics or less obvious psychographics. Some business-oriented B2B service providers go after companies in their communities where it is easy to determine who and how to contact them (just walk in the door or find them on the chamber of commerce website).

Redefining and refining our niches are generally positive moves, keeping our businesses vital and our own mojo alive and well.

Helpful hint: Select a niche in which you can make a living.

Here's a lesson I've learned the hard way: As you refine your niche, select one in which you feel comfortable charging an attractive fee for your work.

My own freelance niche is writing and market research in the insurance and asset management industries. Over the years I've tried focusing on several other areas. I'll discuss two here that did not pan out because I could not bring myself to charge a fair rate consistently. Though my line of work may be far different from yours, you may see similarities between my general situation and yours.

The first problem niche was writing résumés. There's a great need out there, but unfortunately, many of the people who need résumés also need hours of career counseling and confidence building. Furthermore, it takes a lot of interviewing, conceptualizing, wordsmithing, and proofreading to write a good résumé.

An online information publisher sells a product that teaches résumé writing. The sales page claims that résumé writing is a great way to make money fast. You'll be deluged with work because so many people are looking for a job.

So take your fee, multiply by the number of résumés you can write per day (which they allow you to believe is a substantial number), multiply that by the number of days in a week, and multiply that by the number of weeks in a year. Well, you can see the pattern. Simple mathematical equations that build upon themselves will make you rich, just as someone would be a billionaire today if only he had invested a penny in a passbook savings account in the year 1 A.D.

The central challenge in résumé writing is how much to charge clients so you will earn sufficient income for your expertise and time.

Here are two solutions:

Some professional résumé writers (yes, there are credentials for résumé writers) sell an expensive package that includes substantial career coaching.

Others write the résumé for a predetermined fee. If the client then needs help on what to do with this résumé, they sell an additional coaching service separately. If the client doesn't pay for the add-on, he gets the résumé itself but no advice.

So in real life you need a pricing plan that pays for your work . . . even if you are not comfortable quoting a substantial price to unemployed and underemployed people.

Consider the people I call "Girl Scouts." They advise away, justifying an enormous expenditure of unpaid time as "customer service." They hope this wonderful customer service will cause the client to refer others, who in turn will also get much more time and wisdom from the résumé writer than they paid for.

I discovered my inner Girl Scout. I realized I would need to completely change my way of thinking and billing to succeed in this business. Rather than make this change, I refocused on insurance and financial writing.

I have also worked on websites and other marketing materials for struggling entrepreneurs.

You may notice a pattern here. Résumé clients and entrepreneurs are both looking for work but may not have any paying work at this time. Both present fascinating marketing challenges that can fuel hours of fact-finding and discussion. But if you don't have the guts to require payment for all the hours you work, you're a Girl Scout.

I was guilty as charged.

Even when I had an agreement to be paid by the hour, I'd find myself whittling down records of actual time spent so I would not feel uncomfortable sending the invoice.

Now I am convinced that insurance and financial services are my industries. They are right for me because I am comfortable charging an adequate fee. Sometimes I still experience sticker shock as I prepare an estimate. That's one way I know I've found the right solopro niche.

For additional perspective, ask yourself questions along these lines: *How long has the company postponed the project waiting for an employee to find the time to complete it? What would another experienced freelancer charge? What is the annual salary of the individual at this company who is contracting for my work?*

In the case of my clients, I assume that someone who has the authority to contract with me makes a bare minimum of $50,000 a year, and I suspect that many of them earn into the six figures. My assignment may cost no more than the shrimp cocktail and expensive alcohol they serve at insurance agents' golf outings.

It's not just what the folks hiring you earn. The company runs many of its calculations in the millions of dollars.

Ah, that helps.

In summary, if you are a Girl Scout at heart (and for purposes of this discussion, boys can certainly be Girl Scouts), don't select a service that tempts you to charge low for lots of work. You'll end up with an overwhelming, underpaying workload.

How do I describe what I do so people will beg me to help them solve their problem?

Getting solopro work at a company is about quickly demonstrating that you have the specific knowledge and expertise to do the work a client needs done without much guidance and oversight from them. They may not quiz you about your capabilities as they would in a typical hiring situation, but they must believe you can do the work by the deadline in the isolation of your office, which quite probably is a desk in your home.

Here you need solid qualifications rather than sizzle. These qualifications may consist of credentials, college degrees, years of work experience, membership in professional organizations, awards, experience at a well-known, market-share leader in your industry, or portfolio samples. You also have to be able to tell your story quickly. Try to say it in six words or less.

For instance, I write about insurance for the insurance industry and I have two designations demonstrating expertise. I'll tell prospects that I'm a freelance writer and researcher with CPCU and CLU (insurance industry credentials).

Don't dumb down a message that is clear to your target market to match some sales expert's opinion of what sounds cool. My credentials tell insurance managers loud and clear that they won't have to teach me how the insurance industry works, and they serve me much better than some glossy but irrelevant claim. While initials after your name are handy in quickly communicating your qualifications, also review your résumé for accomplishments, number of years' experience, or anything else you can claim that conveys competence in a few words.

Prospects want to be sure that I can interview their star agent intelligently and write a ready-to-go article for their agent newsletter by a week from Monday even though they'll be tied up at a conference in Las Vegas next week and un-available to advise me. They want to know that I am just like the people in their office (or better) at certain tasks, not that I "improve the bottom line" or cause the sun to shine. The managers who hire people like us aren't impressed by empty sizzle—they want beefy implementation.

Clear. Clearer. Clarity.

Clarity is your primary criterion for evaluating every market-ing message and marketing conversation. Flashy may be nice, succinct is good too, and cute is, well, cute.

But clarity helps you—as well as prospective clients—de-fine what you do. Clarity may sound simple, but it can be deceptively elusive. I've seen people sacrifice clarity and even business positioning to serve a clever play on words.

Here are some possible problems:

- **Boasting about how you generate profits when in reality your services don't generate profits di-rectly.** Plenty of perfectly valid work doesn't clearly show up on the bottom line although well-meaning but naïve advice-givers will tell you that managers want hard-nosed people who bring in money.

- Back when you ran for grade school treasurer you may have won the election by promising to bring more money into the treasury, but in fact, the trea-surer's job is to manage funds, not create them. That holds true in the real world too. Only make claims that are valid for the work you do.

- **Using words with multiple meanings in ways that people don't know what you're talking about.** I'm a "writer" for insurance companies, but if I say that I "write insurance," then I may be interpreted as being in sales or underwriting. I can more correctly call myself a "copywriter," but some people in the insurance industry don't know what a copywriter is. It's a challenge.

- **Using phrases that are cute but don't convey much.** To continue with examples related to writing, I've seen many writers with clever taglines playing with how "write" and "right" sound alike. It has already been done a lot! If you are starting down this road, try to proceed with taste and meaning.

Clarity will always serve you well. But sometimes it proves elusive. Proceed as best you can while you continue to think it through. If you're like most people, you can't afford to postpone marketing activities until your message is perfect.

Have you heard of "virtual assistants"? It may be your answer.

You did many things well at your last good job and you're proud of your contribution to the success of your company. You have a lot of corporate experience. You carried out administrative or technical projects and worked independently. You coordinated complex programs, moved them along, functioned as a team player. In other words, you've advanced the work of your employer and earned your pay.

Still, after reading the last section on clarity, you may be puzzled and even discouraged. You can't quite figure out what career identity it all adds up to. You're uncertain how your what-I-do-well list translates into a freelance or consulting practice. It seems scattered and the achievements are hard to measure. Not like the fabulous sales figures and stirring project management achievements that make for compelling examples in the résumé and website-writing books.

Becoming a virtual assistant may be just right for you.

"What's a virtual assistant?" you may ask. Well, *virtual* means taking place in cyberspace and *assistant* means, well, one who provides assistance. Like in an office, except working from your home computer, even thousands of miles from the client.

VAnetworking.com defines a virtual assistant as "a highly-trained independent entrepreneur who provides a myriad of business support services virtually via phone, fax, and Internet-based technology to support and meet the growing needs of businesses worldwide. ... A VA is your right-hand person helping you to succeed in your business. The irony is you may never meet your VA as odds are they live nowhere near you."

Virtual assistants do all sorts of things, working as executive assistants, administrators, and technicians. They are doers with specialties ranging from data entry and bookkeeping to medical transcription, web design, publicity, social media, creating slide shows in PowerPoint, etc., etc., etc. For more on virtual assistants, see Appendix 2.

To the point:

- To get started as a freelancer or consultant, you'll need to determine what services you offer and to whom you offer them.

- Solopros continue to redefine their niches throughout their careers, so don't aim for perfection. Make a decision and reconsider it as needed.

- If possible, start with a niche that is similar to your last good job.

- The best marketing messages are absolutely clear with no ambiguity about what you do.

- Virtual assistants are solopros who provide business support services from their own locations via technology.

Step 3

Take a Grown-Up Approach to Marketing

The beginning of a new business is all about marketing. If you have no assignments yet, you'll have plenty of free time to land clients. Still, it's vitally important to use this time wisely. Don't piddle the hours away on tasks that absorb lots of time but won't pay off for months or even years.

Many solopros brag about their workaholic tendencies and the outlandishly long days they spend at the computer. I suspect that they count all time at their desk as work, whether they are checking Facebook or texting with friends. All sorts of irrelevant fun can be counted as work if you call it networking.

But adults who are more dedicated to bringing in income than playing at the office concentrate on marketing that gets results as quickly as possible. As you obtain paying work, meeting client deadlines will be your highest priority.

Still, you can never stop marketing. As paid work claims more time, you'll want to balance this work with your marketing activities so there's always an inflow of new assignments with steady income.

This chapter encourages you to think like a mature marketer willing to do what it takes to build a business rather than a hobbyist falling for each marketing fad. Plus it answers some of the questions you may be asking about marketing . . . or will soon ask.

What is the single most important question to ask in evaluating your marketing efforts?

First, the answer: *Am I undertaking this specific activity because I believe it will be the most effective step in building my business, given the time, money, and talents available to me at this time?* Then, its corollary: *Or, am I choosing this technique in deference to my inner weenie?*

Remember, no guts, no glory. Only by doing what works, and works well, will you, well, get work.

If you read professional online forums (e.g., LinkedIn groups), you'll see people embarking on email campaigns in the mid of night or mounting direct (postal) mail campaigns that are very expensive. Some access companies through corporate websites, blindly sending emails to *info*@addresses. Yikes.

Every business is different, but if you have a talent worth offering and you are selecting prospects thoughtfully, the more direct the contact the better. The better your lead (contact information including name, title or at least department, phone number, email address), the more valuable it is for a multi-pronged attack, that is, phone calling, emailing, and even, possibly, an in-person appointment.

What, no website?

Did you know that there are highly successful freelancers/consultants who have no website? I'm always surprised when I find one, but they're out there. It's impossible to know who they are because, well, they have no website and minimal to nonexistent electronic visibility. The reason they have no website is that they have been in business for a while and always have too much paying work to spend time on a website and other accoutrements of contemporary marketing.

These folks embody the advice above. They discovered what works for them and dropped the rest.

Embrace what does not come naturally.

If phoning is the most effective means of finding buyers for your service, and I'm here to tell you it often is, then you pick up the phone.

If you dread telephoning or any other direct interaction with prospects and clients, consider that it is more efficient to push beyond your comfort zone than to constrict your marketing effort around your fears. *Read that again and let it sink in.*

Start with the hints in this book, get advice and morale boosting from others, and simply do what needs to be done. "Embrace what does not come naturally. Only then will you stop limiting yourself," says the quotation posted to my office wall.

Hiring a coach may help you start phoning. This is a better expenditure than stocking up on stamps or running up huge expenses on overnight shipping or printing. Let's say you spend $250 on a coach to develop your comfort level with phoning, a skill that can continue to bring you clients for the rest of your work life. The same amount of money *may* fund 500 letters, including postage, paper, and toner, but that's merely a one-time effort. The letter-mailing campaign will take more time than phoning because you'll still have to identify who to mail to, and the time required to also write, print, and mail the perfect letter is considerable.

Ask yourself the hard question: Which marketing activity is most likely to bring in business quickly? Don't let your fears fog your analytical instincts.

How can I know what my marketing message is when I'm just getting started?

You don't, at least not at the start, at least not entirely.

It sounds reasonable that you determine your very narrow niche and consistently market to that specific niche all over the place with a consistent message. But this is not your first priority on day one.

Instead, test your niche by going general on marketing tools everyone will see, such as your website (if you have one). Then go specific on spoken communications. That's another reason that phone calling is such a great prospecting technique—you can instantly and tightly target your message to the individual you are calling. Let websites, brochures, business cards, voicemail answering messages, and the like be much broader.

You may be thinking of producing different websites and business cards for each niche or specialty. This will drive you crazy. What message do you record on your voicemail intro? Which business card do you hand out at general marketing events? Do you reconsider which signature to use on every email you send? How many different business cards do you carry in your wallet or purse? Aaack!

Just go general with marketing media that can't be customized for the individual recipient. This includes print and websites. For instance, I do both marketing research and marketing communications, primarily in the insurance industry, but also for financial firms as well as companies of all types that I've picked up along the way. Therefore, much of my print marketing, both hard copy and electronic, touts *writing and research: insurance, financial, and business.*

Over time you may wish to add pages to your website that address specific niches.

Aiming for absolute consistency and perfect knowledge at the beginning is exhausting and demanding. Save this for later, much later. Perhaps never.

Reason is on the side of consistency, but practicality and reality allow for varying degrees of specificity. Some day in the future if you define a precise niche, you can go back and align everything with it.

How do I keep the work flowing in?

To maintain optimal work load, you need to keep marketing. Consistent, real-effort, high-returns marketing. This is difficult to do when you are swimming in work, but a successful solopro building a smooth-running operation and wanting to live with minimal stress needs to keep an eye on the future.

So, *do* you have any work lined up for when your current rush project is completed? If not, resign yourself to another round of intensive, fresh-start prospecting when you're done or start doing some easier marketing now, for instance, a few phone calls a day.

Many experts recommend going whole hog all the time. While this may win the undying admiration of fellow travelers down the solopro road in your professional LinkedIn groups, it is totally out of touch with real life. When you are under tight time constraints, your first responsibility is to meet your obligations to clients, not to look for more work. A one-person business cannot keep adding on daily marketing tasks and giving them top priority while consistently meeting promises to clients. Only those without enough paying assignments can engage in such ideal behaviors.

When you start out, it's easy to set goals and objectives and make timelines and establish your blog with but a single entry and commit to various marketing projects. If all these projects bomb and win you no business, you can continue to implement the ideal marketing program full-time, unencumbered with other tasks.

However, let's think positive. If you are undertaking an ambitious marketing program, you will obtain some paying clients. The more you market, the more clients you should obtain. On top of that, as you work for clients, you should obtain repeat business. (Remember that past clients are your most important sources of work over time.) So your work load continues to grow from new business and repeat clients.

Now if you have totally committed yourself to intense marketing on a daily basis, this will take another chunk of time.

Statistically, it simply doesn't work. The time you allot to marketing is substantial and your assignment load is growing. At some point, you simply don't have enough time. It makes no sense to turn down assignments so you can meet the marketing burden you have placed on your own shoulders (unless there is something preferable about the prospects you are seeking relative to the clients you already have).

Marketing a freelance/consulting practice is a balancing act. You must manage the marketing side of the teeter-totter so your to-do list doesn't take over the time necessary for carrying out assignments.

On the other hand, when an assignment is over, it's *over.* One day you are frantically multitasking to meet a deadline and the next you have absolutely nothing to do. It's an unsettling sensation and one that can be partly avoided by marketing all the time . . . but at a carefully considered pace.

What is the most important source of work?

The answer: Repeat assignments from current clients. This gets little attention in marketing books because you don't need to hire a marketing consultant (hopefully) to tell you how to retain clients. You already have the inside track there.

Marketing to new prospects is the second most important source. Of course, if you don't have any clients yet, it's the only source.

Should I, can I, pay someone else to do my marketing?

A popular recommendation is to hire someone to handle your marketing. Let's just agree that almost all of us should focus on making more money from our businesses than we spend on them. Employees, even part-time and virtual ones, can be major drains on your money, and managing them can claim substantial shares of your time and focus.

It depends on your situation, of course, but until you have a solid marketing system, how can you teach another person to implement it? And some activities, such as phoning, are more effective when you do them yourself. There's a world of difference between talking to a business owner who understands every aspect of his work and listening to a scripted robot-person.

What do I do when someone asks me to do work I've never done before?

It happens all the time, but when you first contact prospects for freelance and consulting assignments, it's really surprising when someone asks if you do types of work you have never done before. (This should serve to remind you that there are lots of people out there with hiring budgets who need all sorts of help, and they may be quite inclined to give work to the next person who offers assistance and who seems remotely qualified.)

If you come from a payroll job, your recent experience is industry specific and generally rather intense in a single function. You may be part of a large team, but your task is limited to twisting in Phillips screws only.

As a solopro, you may start out with a rather broad specialty despite expert advice to select a narrow niche. Over time you most likely will constrict your horizons, recognizing that this focuses your marketing and justifies a higher fee. At the same time, once you get people to talk to you on the phone, they'll ask you about all sorts of services they need done that you have never considered.

How you handle this is a real judgment call. Generally, I recommend faking a little more confidence than you feel and going for it. Believing in your talents and taking reasonable risks are intrinsic to freelancing and consulting. So, commit and then do everything you need to do to pull off the assignment. Dig out old textbooks, cruise the Internet, phone other professionals for advice, read, practice, buy training materials, call former coworkers. Prepare to spend a lot of unpaid time on the project if necessary. (This last suggestion is definitely a judgment call. It depends on whether you have the time available and if this is how you choose to use it.)

For instance, the first time I was invited to write a feature story for a trade magazine in the insurance industry, I recognized it as a major opportunity but one for which I had no experience. True, I had read a lot of magazine features, but all my writing had been corporate research reports or marketing communications. I had never done an interview-based feature. Though I was fearful, I knew I could pull it off. I accepted the assignment and effortlessly lined up an in-person interview with the target CEO. (Yes, I was blessed.)

To get myself in the groove, I needed to take concrete action. I tape recorded the interview and then transcribed it myself word by word. Then I maintained the best quotations and rephrased the rest so it wouldn't sound like a transcript. Through multiple drafts I kept reworking it until I had created a true feature.

This took a huge amount of time, way more than a seasoned professional would require. But at the time, I told no one that this was such a challenge for me. By the time I submitted my first draft to the editor, it was highly professional. The pay was the publication's standard article rate, but if calculated on a per hour basis, it was abysmal due to my inexperience and my time-consuming approach. Still, the project gave me a prestigious piece for my portfolio and the confidence to go after other magazine assignments.

On the other hand, don't undertake what you are truly unqualified to do. The project may go very badly and you will lose the opportunity to do what you excel at for that client. Also, you will suffer tremendously until you complete or give up on the work.

When you are hopelessly in doubt, here's a good middle way that works for most situations: "I have never done that specific type of work before, but I would like to try it. I have done XYZ so I do have relevant skills in place. How does that sound to you?"

Then listen. You'll have your answer.

What should I do if I am offered a single project that will demand all my time over an extended—but limited—period of time?

Some experienced freelancers/consultants would turn down the project. Even if it pays well, uses their strongest competencies, and sounds like "fun." Honest!

That doesn't mean *you* should turn it down, especially if you are just starting out, but do consider how you are going to prepare for the day when the assignment ends. Or simply acknowledge that once the gig is up, you will eventually be marketing full-time again and budget your finances accordingly.

How can too much of a good thing be pretty bad?

As you may recall, the much quoted Mae West said that too much of a good thing can be wonderful.

But when it comes to freelancing and consulting, too much of a good thing can be a nightmare, especially when that good thing is work. Too much work can take lots of forms, such as too much work in too short a time frame or too much work in total, consisting of too many smaller assignments from too many clients.

The former—too much work from a single client—can have far more damaging repercussions down the road. I have seen freelancers in online forums who berate themselves for not marketing full speed while simultaneously serving a single full-time client for a year or more. Their self-flagellation may seem unreasonable to us, but then, it's easiest to be unreasonable towards ourselves.

For instance, a consultant, upon completing a three-year assignment, found himself idle, and he's been in this sad state for six months. What could he have done differently? He could have consistently marketed for the three years.

That's what forum participants remind such individuals. Sounds good but it doesn't really work. Effective marketing takes time and consistency, and if you are doing a demanding, full-time assignment, you don't have time to market consistently.

And what if you *do* manage to carve out a few hours per

week to market? There's the risk you may quickly land a second assignment. What if you get more work one month into the three years? You can't put off the second client for two years and eleven months, can you?

You could send the offer on to someone else as a favor, but then why bother with the marketing? Or you could take a commission and send it on, but that may give you unwanted supervisory responsibility, depending on how the transaction is managed.

You could take on more work on the side, but can you really pull it off? Work requires creativity and attention to detail—in other words, professionalism—which means you must be rested and alert. If you take on more than you can handle well, you are shortchanging your primary client, your side client or both. And enjoying life less.

Instead, you can gear up your marketing towards the end of the assignment. You still may have the problems above, but not as acutely. Ideally, you may move seamlessly from one client to the next. This is much easier when you are sure of the end date for the original assignment. It is even easier if the first assignment tapers off at the end instead of abruptly concluding.

Or you can prepare in advance for the assignment's completion by saving money and planning ahead for future marketing. This may mean an online newsletter, website, mail campaign, or other labor-intensive re-start-up that you can prepare on the side and then roll out big time when the extended project is completed.

You can charge a surcharge throughout the extended duration of your full-time assignment. However, this may feel counterintuitive when you accept the first offer. You may be tempted to bid low since you won't have to invest time in marketing for quite a while and can relax into the temporary security.

Or you can turn down the assignment. When new to freelancing, it is difficult to contemplate such a thing. But it has been done.

Three years is an exceptionally long project. Many extended assignments aren't quite *that* extended. Full-time assignments lasting several months entail similar decisions, but these decisions are even harder to make. Three years from today seems so far off that you believe you don't need to contemplate at the beginning how to turn on the work stream again. On the other hand, six months is long enough to peer into the future yet too far off to juggle multiple clients for the duration.

Learn from my sad story. I once had what I understood to be a part-time, daily assignment. I gladly accepted rather low pay because it was income I could count on and I needed the work.

The client estimated three hours of work per day and that some days would only take two hours. (This was before I recognized that three billable hours is a lot of time. A regular work day does not have eight billable hours, it has more like four or five.)

The assignment was to turn industry news into an online intelligence service for a large corporation. As a cost-saving move, the client had cancelled subscriptions that would yield content, and based on initial conversations, I expected that less information meant less work for me to do.

But it turned out that less information readily provided meant more research and more work on my end. Oops! After about a month I resigned that assignment and wallowed in the relief . . . except that I had slacked off on marketing.

Moral of the story: Know what you are getting into and what you may be giving up. All that glitters may not be as golden as it first appears.

I'm desperate for work. Should I ask one person for a freelance and a full-time job at the same time? Should I plead for any work I can get?

Sounds efficient, right?

Let's say that your goal is simply to work in your chosen field. And to earn an income doing it. As soon as possible. Let's add that you are pursuing this work by telephoning the people most likely to help you—executives and managers at sizable companies.

If you have gotten through by phone to someone who has the standing to hire you for a freelance assignment and they are engaging you in conversation and they seem friendly and interested, you are probably itching to ask if they have full-time openings. After all, they may be a day away from posting the perfect job for you, and since you are talking directly with a decision maker, you have the inside track. Right?

Uh, sorry, but probably wrong.

Let's try again.

This morning you looked at your checkbook and it's in a really sorry state. You maintain your professionalism while asking on the phone about assignments. They are receptive but don't immediately give you work. So you confide that you are in desperate straits and will take anything they can scrape up for you to do, regardless of how little the pay.

I know you are thinking this sounds absurdly unprofessional, but many of us have been on the brink of doing this very thing. (I know that I have.) Some of us have actually broken down and pleaded. (Thankfully, I have not.)

I'm not saying that these strategies never work. Everything works sometimes. But both are more likely to backfire than succeed. In the first story you warn the prospect that you may walk away from freelancing as soon as you get a *real* job. In the second story, you appear too frantic to do the work in a professional manner. In other words, there's TMI (too much information!) here.

To succeed as a freelancer, you must consistently present yourself as a prestige professional. Requesting freelance work assignments and full-time employment on the same phone call positions you poorly for both. The pairing demonstrates to prospects that you are not successful . . . and clients are attracted to success, not failure.

There's nothing wrong with doing freelance while you continue to look for a full-time job, just as there's nothing wrong with pursuing big-fish freelance clients while performing the little-minnow assignments currently on hand. Your plans are no business of the client. They are private and speculative at this point. So long as you commit to honoring any contracts for specific assignments, that's all anyone has a right to expect.

Here's another quandary: A corporate client has an opening in your specialty and phones to ask if you are interested. This is not a good omen for you as a freelancer. If they are filling a staff position, they may no longer need your freelance services. So if you are firmly committed to freelancing, resolve to beef up your marketing immediately.

But what if you are truly interested in the position? You appear to have a good chance at it, but proceed with caution. If you say *no thanks*, more than likely your freelance assignments will continue, at least until the position is filled. Express interest and you may get no further assignments. This may, of course, be because the position is soon filled and there is no need for you.

But I think it goes beyond that. Becoming an applicant puts you at a disadvantage for freelance. They may want to cool their freelance relationship with you, believing when they see your name on caller ID that you are following up on your application. Indeed, you are reduced to being simply another job seeker. And if they ultimately give the position to someone else—perhaps an internal applicant with powerful mentors—they will feel uncomfortable working with you. You will be diminished in their eyes from an impressive *consultant* to a sorry reject.

To succeed as a freelancer, you must consistently present yourself as a prestige professional who is their equal (or better). Present yourself as a sad-sack supplicant and opportunities will dry up.

What if I propose solopro work and then they ask if I am available for a "real" job?

If you are totally committed to self-employment along the lines described above, you may believe you must express this commitment before learning the whole story because of *brand consistency* or whatever.

But here's my new answer, delivered with dignity and confidence: "I love freelancing (or consulting), but I am always open to opportunity. And if this opportunity is not right for me, I may know someone else who can benefit from it. So I'd love to hear more."

(Anyway, you are itching to know the pay range, aren't you?)

Solopro versus company employment: Should an economic slump affect my career decision?

I'll take any work I can get is the message most likely to yield no offer at all.

Prepare all your marketing tools, whether for solopro or full-time corporate work, to present yourself in the most positive light and highlight your appeal. In other words, you are a winner. Resolve now to maintain that stance without wavering.

Some solopro freelancers and consultants believe that they are more desirable than the rest of the pack because they have married themselves till death-do-they-part to their business model. They would never stoop to full-time employment. They believe this gives them an edge in getting assignments.

I used to believe this too. I believed that I must irrevocably wed myself to freelancing in order to offer my services with authentic conviction. Demonstrating this devotion doesn't matter to me now, which is kind of curious because I am more certain about self-employment now than I was back when this dilemma absorbed me more deeply.

Individuals who have lost their corporate jobs during an economic downturn ask if they should tell a prospective solopro client that they are also looking for a full-time job. It is eternally true that asking for both makes you less attractive for either. But today there is a new facet to the issue: You don't need to express interest in a full-time job because they already know you are open to it.

How do they know?

By looking at your résumé or LinkedIn profile. Anyone who has been employed consistently for twenty years and is now a solopro can be assumed to want a full-time job if the right one comes along.

It's common sense.

How can I inoculate myself against economic bad news?

Networking with other solopreneurs can be dangerous. You make yourself susceptible to catching the it-won't-work virus from the people you meet. You leave your prospecting tasks behind to go network and find your head nodding sympathetically to accounts of how hard it is to find freelance, no one is hiring, and the rare someone who is hiring expects to pay Third World wages.

Try this: Instead of passively listening to their woes, ask how many people they have contacted. I guarantee that it's fewer than a hundred. Quite possibly they have contacted no one individually and have limited their outreach to email (or even Twitter!) rather than direct phone calls. Worse yet, some people say it's "all about networking" as an excuse to wait for clients to find them!

The problem is them, not the marketplace. This doesn't mean you have to set them straight. Continue nodding but don't take what they're saying to heart. Allow their pity party if you don't feel like confronting them.

How to take the *yuck* out of networking?

By this point it's clear that I endorse telephoning prospects for freelance and consulting work!

You may think that anyone as crass as I am will do *anything* to get paying assignments. But surprisingly, I have my limits. I won't do indiscriminate networking. I don't accost strangers, or even friends and relatives, with my pitch unless I have sufficient reason to believe they or someone they know could benefit from my services.

How about the guy in line behind me at the grocery at 10 P.M. who is buying a case of Bud? Nah.

Or Aunt Edna, who lives in a trailer park sixty miles outside Charleston, West Virginia? Nope.

Or the teenager sitting beside me on the plane, flying to her parents' home in Scarsdale for the holidays? Again, no.

Well, actually this third person is slightly more likely than average to know someone, but I let it go anyway.

The avid networkers out there think there is something wrong with me for phoning strangers. But I think there is something even more bizarre about people who see every human being who crosses their path as a connection.

Have I missed out on opportunities? Perhaps. There's no way of ever knowing. But I'm OK with that. I'd rather lose out on a connection than live my life in perpetual barracuda mode.

What if I find myself in conversation with someone actually likely to hire me? My freelance niche is rather narrow (writing for insurance and asset management companies), but if it happens, I'm prepared. So as soon as I recognize someone as a relevant contact, I bubble up with, "Gee, you're a marketing director at XYZ Insurance Company. That is so cool because I'm a freelance writer and an insurance specialist who writes copy for companies such as yours. Do you ever use freelancers?"

The answer may be *no* or it may be *maybe* or it may even be *yes*! In which case I can ask for her card and propose following up with her when she's back in the office. Then we can return to casual conversation. I don't have to worry about how to enter my services into the conversational flow or pray she'll ask me the right lead-in question.

Life is delightful when you don't live it as a twenty-four-hour cog in the marketing machine.

Why should networking be done differently by solopros than by job hunters?

There are simple, obvious (when you think about it) reasons that networking by solopro freelancers and consultants should be done entirely differently from how those seeking full-time jobs do it.

To set the stage for my observations, please remember that the job (or entrepreneurial) gods don't reward you for frantic effort with little chance of paying off. *It's strategic networking that works.*

Those looking for full-time jobs often seek a position that builds on their experience from their last job and that may be in the same broad category, but they tend to be flexible on industry, niche within the industry, exact duties, etc. depending on the opportunities that present. This makes sense. They will be onsite forty plus hours a week and will soon get up to speed on corporate and industry specifics.

These job seekers narrow their search primarily by travel distance. Certainly a few people are open to moving cross country, but most limit their search to a specified distance from their homes. Some are willing to spend an hour each way driving fifty miles or more, others insist upon walking to work, but either way, they have limits.

On the other hand, today's solopros often work virtually from home with little guidance from clients. At the same time, they want to maximize their pay rates through specialization. Therefore, they search out opportunities that closely match their experience regardless of location.

This makes a world of difference in how job seekers and solopros network.

The common wisdom in conducting a corporate job hunt is to tell everyone you know that you are looking. Not coincidentally, most of the people you know live in your community. They are most likely to identify leads in close proximity to you. If the job differs somewhat from what you've done in the past, not a problem (except perhaps in a very tight, inflexible job market).

In contrast, telling everyone you know exactly what you do can be exhausting and unproductive when you solopro. Your acquaintances don't know what a DC-483X is and they still don't know after you explain it. You are needlessly draining your energy in pursuing contacts that won't pay off. People whose relationship with you is based largely on physical nearness often cannot help you no matter how much they would like to.

The local chamber of commerce may have no other members in your profession or industry. Even your local professional organization may not be sufficiently narrow in its focus. Instead, save your networking money for the annual conference of a highly targeted organization, even if the event is hundreds of miles away.

What *benefit* should I never sell?

I see many websites for freelancers/consultants that offer the same benefit, and every time I see this benefit I cringe: By using a freelancer you can save money on vacation time, health insurance, and other benefits. Achieve *staffing flexibility*. Use my services only as needed and save money the rest of the time!

I confess. I also used this benefit in selling my services during the 1990s, and my first website, posted in 1998, centered this benefit on the home page. However, now you see this nowhere on my website and I've permanently retired this text. Here's why:

It has a hint of martyrdom. It's like saying, *go ahead, exploit me.* I don't expect the same benefits your other workers are receiving. I'm here to be treated poorly.

You're a pro and an expert so expect the best, not the worst. That's starts with your rate. It's high. Clients are not paying for your personnel benefits directly. Instead, they are paying a higher hourly rate (though perhaps technically based on a measurement other than by the hour) to compensate in part for those benefits not directly billed. Anyway, the point is that you are outstanding in the quality of your services and therefore command top rates.

Every prospect is well aware of this so-called benefit of using independent workers. The era has long passed when we had to educate prospects about this basic concept. We are professionals and deserve all the financial and other benefits the word implies. We freelance and consult because we have superior skills that enable us to advise others wisely and to implement independently. We hold our services in high esteem and expect to be paid accordingly.

Our rates sound high, and they should sound high. We have invested years of study and experience to attain such high levels of performance. And not incidentally, we devote hours of unpaid time to prospecting, preliminary research, administrative tasks, etc.

In writing marketing emails, websites, etc., is there such a thing as too long?

This may not be a first-day-of-business question. But as you work on your website, emails, etc., you'll ask yourself this question constantly. That's because when you ask for feedback from family and friends, they'll tell you it's too long. Most people will tell you most everything you write is too long. That's because you're asking people to read your stuff for free and they are not real prospects.

Real prospects who are thinking of paying money for your services want to know as much as possible about you before they work with you. They're really interested. They aren't bored unless it's poorly written or *really* boring.

Therefore, the more you tell, the more you sell. That's a copywriting maxim. Not original to me. Your communication objective is clarity. Clarity may require quite a few words. Clarity requires specificity.

Does this advice apply to telephoning? Yes, and to voice-mail messages as well. Don't worry about length. It's more important to tell clients what they need to know from your message. Talk slowly and clearly, especially when leaving phone numbers or email addresses. Repeat your name and phone number at the beginning and at the end so they can jot it down without replaying it.

Believe me, no one is intrigued sufficiently by vagueness or empty sizzle to track you down and get an explanation. If you mumble your phone number, the rest of the effort is wasted. Sure, they may be able to look up your phone number on their cell phone, but most people won't bother.

So tell it well. Don't multitask. When you are making calls, don't read your email, wipe up the crumbs from your donut, do crosswords, watch TV, or discipline the kids at the same time. And don't go looking for the next number you'll call. Focus. The voicemails I leave new prospects *always* take longer than sixty seconds.

Everyone will tell you that people today have no patience for wordiness. They want instant info. MTV. Texting. Just the facts. That's true for others but not for you. You have carefully selected names to contact because you believe your services will help these people. When people find something that will help them, they want to know about it.

If you are bald, you'll listen to a half-hour commercial for Rogaine. If you have a full head of hair, ten seconds is too long and dull. So if your prospects are pulling out their hair in desperation (clever, huh?), you're not too long. Nor do you need to pad your call with small talk and drivel. If they need help, their need for your service is more interesting than impending rain.

Of course, some people aren't interested in your service. Next!

How do I use the input of friends?

With caution. It's not like they're experts in your work or even in general marketing. Listen with an open mind, avoid being too sensitive and defensive, and consider what they say. Don't feel compelled to take their advice. You bring your career experience to your decisions. You've been surfing the web, talking to others, reading, and most important, thinking.

Don't give your opinions second-rate standing in homage to theirs.

Handwritten notes? Maybe not.

A recurring theme in small-business marketing advice is that you should send handwritten notes. Lots of notes! Carry the blanks in your briefcase and get them in the mail anytime anyone contacts you or achieves something or you think something nice about them.

Marketers tell us to handwrite thank yous after sales presentations and job interviews. Write each individual who sat in on the presentation separately, by hand. Seems like a nice personal touch.

But wait! Let's think about this for a moment. Some of these notes are not mere thank yous. They are full-blown sales letters. They have a mission far beyond thanking. They reiterate what we want to emphasize from the meeting, expand upon themes we want to flesh out, follow up with additional thoughts or information, or specify how we will continue to follow up.

Though I myself have written very long letters in the past, I now think it is silly to hand-write a message of more than three sentences.

Long messages with marketing intentions require too much copy to be handwritten. They also require too much

thought and wordsmithing to be tossed off in a single draft—
and copying a draft with nice handwriting is just too tedious.

A lengthy handwritten letter can go two or even three
pages, causing hand cramps.

Handwritten notes recall my childhood.

The first law of our household when I was growing up was
that a handwritten thank you note must be sent promptly
when any gift is received. It must have at least three sentences,
it must be written in good-girl script, and the child must address the envelope him/herself so that the recipient sees no
evidence of adult enforcement.

We would sit at the kitchen table writing mom's dictation while she cooked. As the years went by (yes, we were
slow learners, but then again, the standards were sky high),
we gradually internalized phrases such as *I appreciate your
thoughtfulness* and *I will use your generous gift toward my college
education*. Eventually we wrote notes on our own.

I would picture Emily Post or Mamie Eisenhower, seated
in a shirtwaist dress and pearls, writing with a Cross fountain
pen on refined Crane stationery, and I reluctantly carried on
the tradition.

My brother and I would keep in mind that the income
earned per hour of thank you writing made it a lucrative activity, but still, our hearts would fill with dread as the mailman
(they were all men back then) dropped off thick stacks of en-
velopes when graduation or religious ceremonies approached.

Practice makes perfect. So I learned to write notes the hard
way.

I'm now highly proficient at getting the suckers into the
mail quickly. To this day I continue to write nice notes with
tremendous speed. They are composed in an attractive, femi-
nine hand, written in straight lines.

But I seldom handwrite notes related to my business.

How to send word-processed letters?

Obviously, handwritten notes must be sent via postal mail. But what to do with word-processed correspondence?

Opinion varies. There's something nice and tangible about a letter on nice stationery with a pretty stamp. However, for work purposes I usually favor corresponding by email. I like the way my letter arrives immediately. And it simply makes sense for a message composed on an electronic device to be delivered via technology.

Still, it is impossible to know what's happening at the other end. Some people even send the same letter in both formats. This is acceptable if you alert the recipient to the duplication in both versions so you don't appear to be absentminded.

Some people write their thank you in advance of an in-person meeting, store it on their laptop, and email it from the lobby before leaving the building. Never ever ever do this! It communicates loud and clear that you are sending a form letter that was not customized to reflect what actually happened in the meeting.

To the point:

- As your business develops, carrying out paid assignments will have top priority. However, you must also market consistently to ensure steady work and steady income.

- The most important marketing idea is the one that brings in the most high-quality work for the least expenditure of resources. In real life, this often means phoning.

- If you can't pinpoint a single marketing message, vary

your message to match each individual you phone and generalize your message for all media that are not one-on-one. Technically this will result in inconsistencies, but it avoids the craziness of managing too many conflicting messages.

- Do not actively pursue solopro assignments and full-time employment with the same individual.

- This chapter deals with all sorts of questions and situations that can't be summarized. Sorry. So bookmark it to read later if you don't want to take time for it now.

Step 4

Say "Hi" to Our Friend the Phone

At this point you're thinking you *should* do phone calls but it's not for you. You don't know what to say. What if they ask a hard question? You're feeling as awkward as you were at your first sixth-grade dance.

Fortunately, we're not school kids any more. We talk on the phone every day for diverse professional and private purposes. Our objectives and our opinions often prevail though we don't recognize these occasions as the sales calls they are.

You can do this. You don't need a high-pressure sales rap. Simple conversation works just fine.

Yes, people get lots of calls from near strangers and absolute strangers, but most of these calls are tightly scripted and don't connect with the recipients.

You're different. You are calling to offer help and you are not manipulating people to say "yes" against their will.

Here's how to do it.

What should I say when I phone a prospect?

Telephoning for freelance or consulting assignments is a straight-forward task. You ask if they use freelancers (or consultants) and offer your services. Yes, it's that simple. There is no magic phrase or word that opens all doors and transforms people into putty in your hand.

You dial. Someone answers. You ask for the person.

If they identify themselves upon answering, listen to their name. Do they call themselves Charles or Chuck? Write it down.

Then you introduce yourself and briefly present either your relation to them or your qualifications. This is typically half a sentence showing that you know them, belong to the same professional organization, share a friend, or simply that you have expertise in their industry, perhaps developed while working at a competitor or attaining a specific license or professional designation. Explain that you freelance (or consult) in whatever service you offer and ask if they use freelancers (or consultants).

Here is a typical script I use in calling prospects in the marketing departments of U.S. insurance companies for copywriting assignments:

> *Hi, Chuck, This is Diana Schneidman. I'm an experienced insurance copywriter with a CLU and CPCU and I'm calling to see if you use freelancers for your writing needs. (Note: CLU stands for Chartered Life Underwriter and CPCU stands for Chartered Property/Casualty Underwriter, well-known industry designations indicating years of insurance-industry experience.)*

How to proceed with the conversation

If they say yes, they use freelancers, explain that you are interested in assignments with them and ask how to proceed.

If they say no, they'll probably say why. Ask if they have considered using freelancers. Or maybe they'll ask a different question, such as what kind of work you do or if you have samples available.

You continue the conversation as it develops, obviously without a script. This may seem scary at first, but after decades of phone experience dating back to your toddler years, you'll quickly develop answers to their questions.

Try to give prospects the link to your website, LinkedIn profile, or other representations of who you are so they can keep you on file. Volunteer to send an email with appropriate links so they can look you up. (See the Appendix for one of my typical emails.)

If they suggest a possible future project but are not ready to proceed at this time, ask when they may be ready to go ahead with it and note this in your calendar for callback.

Soon you'll have a feel for the expectations of your industry. For instance, the marketing executives in the insurance industry whom I call go prickly if you offer a slick USP (Unique Selling Proposition). They detest perky and sales-y, especially if I suggest meeting with them in person or talking further to propose a new marketing idea that will *improve the bottom line* or *take your sales to the next level.*

They have decades of experience and don't expect to hear anything they haven't heard before. They want to get down to business and prevent unnecessary meetings.

In summary, telephoning for assignments is a simple, direct process. It quickly becomes comfortable if you plan in advance how you will initiate the conversation.

Whatever happens in the conversation, offer to send a brief email that introduces your services, with a link to your LinkedIn profile, website, blog, or whatever. And then send it out immediately!

The best telephone script? It's the one you feel most comfortable delivering.

If you set out to use allegedly no-fail, pin-'em-down-every-time language in your sales telephoning because some expert says you should, and if you cringe when you say it—even if you deliver the lines as professionally as an actor would—you will find every excuse in the world to quit phoning.

When you work for yourself, you are the boss. You are not confined to a phone bank with rusty ashtrays, Styrofoam cups of coffee, and scheduled shifts. You don't have a boss listening in on your calls and critiquing them in stern performance appraisals.

You are the judge and jury, and with every cringe-inducing line you recite, you become more desperate to escape the trap you yourself have set. You may feel called to do the breakfast dishes or sort the recyclables from the rest of the trash. You may tune in to *The View* or fall victim to a sudden headache. You may even resort to assembling tax records. After all, is there any activity more tedious, and therefore nobler, than making sense of your receipts?

Remember that no matter what you say on the phone, large percentages of people you call will not buy your services today. No matter how skillfully you develop the conversation and pressurize the *close*, only a small percentage of calls will yield assignments.

Success is in the numbers. Telephoning to offer professional services is about identifying the relatively small percentage of target companies that may be interested in the type of services you offer and then actually making the calls! Anything that keeps you from making large numbers of calls impedes your success.

Sure, with experience you'll feel comfortable trying out new lines. But you will never have slam dunk results that positively prove that aggressive scripts save the day.

Instead, since it's the numbers that work, you must make every effort to maintain your motivation to make sufficient calls. And nothing will destroy morale and deter you from phoning more than feeling pressured to deliver a yucky sales pitch by a self-proclaimed expert on the Internet or in a book.

It's the act of making calls that creates success much more assuredly than any specific, catchy word or line.

So let yourself off your own hook. Develop a sales conversation that makes you feel good and you'll find it much easier to do phoning.

Know, like, and trust: Why is trust the greatest of these?

The *1 Corinthians* trinity of faith, hope, and charity is slightly better known, but then it has a two millennia head start over the "know, like, and trust" mantra of virtually (a pun, sorry) every expert on Internet marketing.

The authorities preach that *knowing* and *liking* must precede *trusting*, but that hasn't been my experience as a freelancer. I've found it easy to skip directly to trust. And to me, establishing trust is the essence of what I'm doing when I call prospects.

You can have trust without the client knowing and liking you all that much. It happens every day. Consider what happens when phoning for assignments: You start with little to no chitchat—not even *how's the weather, how's the football team* (if you are drawn to that sort of thing)—and then you get down to business, explaining briefly what you do and asking for gigs.

Even in this preliminary phase of the phone call you can start establishing trust. As you succinctly describe your services, credentials, past employers, industry memberships, etc., feel free to use jargon and acronyms that your listener will readily understand. This creates rapport and assures the person on the other end of the line that you are an industry insider . . . and that it's the same industry as theirs.

When they hire a freelancer, clients want to feel very much like they are working with an in-house employee who is already up to speed on the specifics of the work.

How often should I call prospects?

Recently I reconnected with a long-ago acquaintance dating back to my life in the early 1990s. Finding Susan, a fellow freelancer, brought back a lot of old memories. In particular, I called her for advice when I first started as a freelance writer—and one piece of her wisdom has stayed with me vividly all this time.

Let's back up here. I phoned her religiously every day for a week and left a message on her answering machine each time without hearing back. Having recently left corporate employment and being new to phoning as a marketing practice, I began to feel that I was superb at follow-up and highly responsible, while she was negligent and sloppy. I'll be more successful than she has been, I smugly thought.

The next week she finally called me back, indignant that I had left so many messages. She had been out of town and had listened to her answering machine, but she couldn't call back until she got home. She warned me that possible clients would be turned off at receiving so many calls spaced so tightly.

I took her advice to heart and scaled back on my persistence, realizing that what I thought looked so good was casting me as a *nudnik* (pest) or worse in the eyes of others.

When calling for freelance assignments, I now go for quantity of initial contacts over multiple contacts of one individual.

If I am especially interested in a certain prospect or they have requested my call, I may do two or three calls spaced three days apart. For a contact of slightly lesser importance, I'll do a second call one week later. And for many contacts, I will reach out to them once every six weeks to two months (or less frequently if I am busy with paying work).

I see a lot of assertive marketing in a competitive environment, and speaking as a buyer as well as a seller of B2B services, it seems to be based on a misconception: The person called is under some type of obligation to buy your service—or at least hear out your entire spiel—because you have decided that they must do so.

You may call this persistence or being conscientious or something along those lines. I call it a nuisance. Except when it becomes especially overbearing. Then I call it stalking.

I once attended a seminar at which the speaker recommended that you phone every day into eternity until the contact either takes the desired action or tells you to quit calling. Wow. Talk about inviting rejection. Some people deserve every bit of rejection they demand.

Phoning the same person every day is way too aggressive for my taste. Once the person being called feels more like the target of a psychopath than partner to an eventual business transaction, it's over. They may have been somewhat receptive to the first phone message but they didn't call back because they didn't have time right then or they didn't need your service. They may have had it on their to-do list to call later in the week.

But once they get a taste of this harassment, they become more repelled with each call. They may even decide they would never work with you if you were the last person left on earth with your type of expertise.

I heard another technique that is different in the details

but almost as annoying in its implementation. Here's how it works. Say you make your first call on Monday but the intended recipient is not in. (At least you think they are not in. Maybe they are at their desk but not answering calls from names they don't recognize. Such is the delight of caller ID.)

You leave a message saying you will call back in three work days (that is, Thursday) at 9 A.M. You call Thursday and again they do not answer. So you leave a message that you will call back in three work days (Tuesday) at 9 A.M. and you do so. You keep repeating this process until you have called a total of five times, once on each of the five days of the workweek.

This proves you are dependable and assertive, the experts claim. The experts assume that your victim—er, prospect—is powerless in the face of such stick-to-it-iveness and will be putty in your hands.

Now I have to admit that this technique is mathematically appealing. You call on each of the five days of the workweek, and if the sole impediment to your connecting is that the individual is out of the office on certain days, it does resolve that problem.

However, I believe that is rarely the real problem. If someone wants to speak to you, he will get the message and call you back.

And while some messages are quickly deleted or overlooked so that the recipient doesn't recognize that your first follow-up is not your first call, this ceases to be the situation after a few more calls.

There is a perception out there that people can be forced to want you and your services if you monopolize them sufficiently. Phone them repeatedly as misguided proof of your dependability and then verbally wrestle them into submission, says this logic.

Telephoning doesn't have to be that way. Find a technique with which you are comfortable and repeat it with lots of the right people.

I assure you, it works!

What is the best time of day and day of the week to phone a prospect?

The best time to call is when you happen to have the time, have the phone handy, and the setting is quiet. There's no way you can know the best time from their standpoint unless you have supernatural eyesight or contact the best psychic in the world. So why try?

There are a few instances in which you may know the best time. For instance, many stockbrokers prefer to take calls after the New York Stock Exchange closes. But such cases are rare.

Experts claim you should call either before or after standard office hours. They say highly paid executives have achieved their success by working longer hours than everyone else.

I don't buy it. In my office days, I saw many executives who used their power to determine their hours with greater freedom than the underlings. Furthermore, if they stay late, it is expressly to do something specific. Perhaps they are talking to an associate in their office or reading through their inbox or preparing for a presentation.

More than likely, they are not sitting at their desks awaiting an unexpected call. And with caller ID, no one is taking a prospecting phone call that is not convenient. (The occasional exception is when they don't recognize the incoming phone number.) In short, call at the best time for you because you have no way of knowing the best time for them.

I only call during standard business hours because I am

not interested in tricking people into talking to me. I operate from the assumption that if people knew what I was offering, they would be more likely to take my calls, not less likely.

Ya gotta have a certain amount of ego for this kind of work. If you don't, fake it until you do.

Should I leave a voicemail message?

When you start telephoning for work, you will find that many or even most of your calls will roll over to voicemail. Some "experts" recommend hanging up and trying again later. They call repeatedly until they talk to a live person and believe that not leaving voicemails makes them less of a pest.

Instead, I recommend leaving a message . . . always!

If you have something important to say—and you do, or else you wouldn't be calling!—go ahead and say it. Your message is an important opportunity to explain what you do and inform a potential prospect of your services.

With today's communication overload, most business people don't return voicemails that do not clearly identify the caller and the reason for the call. In fact, most people don't return clearly identified calls either. Still, they may listen to the whole message and save your name and phone number for future use even if they don't return your call today.

I've been called back years after my initial phone call. I've even had my information passed on to other companies on the basis of a single voicemail message.

And if you don't leave a message, they certainly won't call back!

Leaving a message helps people who need your help.

Our fundamental marketing belief must be that we offer an

important service. That leads to the practice of only contacting people who may be in the market for this service at some time. Neither our voicemail messages nor our emails, therefore, are ever spam in any sense of the word.

Those people who are interested, because they do need help and it could be from you, want to know as much as possible. You are helping people, not wasting their time! So let's agree that we can leave a long-enough message. Mine typically runs at least sixty seconds. Some close in on two minutes unless the technology cuts me off. (That's why you start with your name and phone number.)

How to combine an email message with a voicemail message

A basic quandary faces those who telephone for freelance or consulting assignments. Should you maintain mystery in the hope that the prospect will call you back to find out why you called? Or should you give enough information so they understand why you called and can make an informed decision about how (or whether) to proceed?

Traditional "cold" calling practice is often to leave a simple call-me-back message when you don't get an answer so the person will be sufficiently intrigued to call back. ("Who is this?" they ask themselves, calling back to relieve the tension of not knowing, goes the logic.)

However, I favor leaving a more complete message because few people are interested enough to call back people whose names they don't recognize. This message will include my phone number and perhaps a URL (website) as well. That's why I like sending an email with my website or LinkedIn link immediately after the call. This way they don't have to write down the website (correctly spelled) while hearing the phone message.

Of course, this only works if you have the prospect's email address or can construct it using the pattern observed on the corporate website.

I am hoping that the person will either listen to the full phone message or read the email. I cross reference the two to avoid confusion and annoying redundancy.

The voicemail message states that I am sending an email that explains a little about how my service may be of use to them.

The subject line of the email may say: Follow up to voicemail: Need help with [XYZ service]?

A checklist for your script when you reach voicemail

- Give your name and phone number, slowly and clearly.

- Tell them where you got their name if it's relevant, such as being a fellow member of a professional organization.

- Explain what you do, emphasizing clarity over the sizzle. (Everyone has a *passion* for whatever they do and *contributes to the bottom line*. So what?)

- Refer them to the email you are sending right now (if you have their email address) or give your website or your name as it appears in your LinkedIn profile slowly and clearly so they can actually visit it.

- Say you would welcome the opportunity to discuss their [fill in the niche] needs.

- Conclude by repeating your name and phone number, slowly, and wrap up the message.

A sample voicemail message

This sample message is from my prospecting days as a freelance writer/marketing researcher specializing in insurance and asset management.

> *Hi, Jim, this is Diana Schneidman at 555.555.5555 in the Chicago area. I am calling you as a fellow member of the Society of Insurance Research. [I was a member at the time.] I am a CLU and a CPCU, and I write marketing research reports for companies such as yours, using either your survey data or by conducting my own print, Internet, and interview research. I'd welcome the opportunity to discuss if my services may benefit your organization. Meanwhile I am emailing you a brief message that explains what I do with links to my website. Again, this is Diana Schneidman at 555.555.5555. I hope we can talk soon. Have a great day.*

So, who is it that I phone for solopro freelance and consulting assignments?

You've wrapped your brain around the idea of targeted calling, or telephoning, the best prospects for freelance or consulting assignments, right? When you are ready to get started or simply ready to think about getting started, another issue presents itself: Whom to call?

Lists range from terrific to terrible. It's easiest to phone large numbers of people if you have a ready-to-go set of ideal names with phone numbers. You'll work your way down the list, phoning and keeping records of contact info and what was said, call by call.

If you already have this list, it's amazing how quickly you'll accomplish your objective. However, in real life you'll almost never find this perfect list. It's more likely that you'll have a quality list that you'll have to weed through for the most appropriate leads.

Free lists

Lists of companies are simple to find. Your public library has electronic databases. Print and online listings abound. There's the chamber of commerce membership directories, the phone directories (online and in print), free newspapers that are thrown in your driveway, and online lists of market-share leading companies by industry. There's LinkedIn, Twitter, and Facebook.

The best names for your purpose may be of mid-level executives. Therefore, databases that do not list individuals below C-level, i.e., Chief Executive Officer, Chief Operations Officer, etc., are not worth your money but are an initial free tool towards finding individuals.

At the nearly worst, you'll have to flesh out a list consisting solely of company names.

Then there's the most challenging task of all: pulling together company names from Google searches, trade journal articles, and whatnot of all types.

This last type of list assembling is best done on an ongoing basis. Scan industry publications or local business weeklies or the city newspaper for lists of hires, promotions, etc. Every time you read or hear of a company or someone to contact, write it down and call the next morning.

The best list has a large percentage of people who represent your target market, both in terms of function or department and in terms of industry. These are the people most likely to offer you assignments. They are also the people most likely to value your services sufficiently to pay top dollar.

Purchased lists

To buy a list or not? The best list provides individuals' names, job titles, direct phone numbers, and email addresses. Do not spend money on a list that does not provide all this data.

And the best source for the best purchased list? Professional and trade association membership directories. You obtain online access (or a print copy) by joining the association. You are not buying a list per se. Instead, you join the organization and obtain the list as a member benefit. Be sure to list this membership on your website, LinkedIn profile, résumé, etc.

To determine if you should join an organization, look online at the list of officers and their work titles. That's a sampling of the group's membership. Or ask current clients and networking contacts which organizations they belong to and recommend.

As I start the phone conversation with a prospect, I say that I am a fellow member of XYZ organization. This warms up the call and positions me as serious about our profession and/or industry.

A possible pitfall. Some organizations specify that their membership list is not to be used for solicitation. As far as I'm concerned, if you belong to an organization and phone another member, you are "networking," not soliciting. And of course, in the off chance the organization gets on your case, threaten not to renew your membership. That should solve the problem.

By the way, this is all theoretical. No one has ever challenged my calling fellow association members, and the vast majority of those who have picked up my call (rather than allowing it to roll over to voicemail) have been very gracious.

After I identify a company, how do I find the right person to phone for freelance or consulting assignments?

When phoning companies for freelance or consulting assignments, it's essential to call the right person. (This response obviously addresses those times you are working from a resource that does not identify personnel by name and title.)

For starters, the right person to talk to is not in Human Resources. True, sometimes when you call the receptionist, they automatically transfer your call to HR to take your application.

Almost every career advisor or résumé writer will tell you to avoid HR like the plague when seeking full-time employment. And how much more true when you solopro! Some HR contacts will take your info, though I doubt that they know what to do with it. Other HR phone answerers will confidently assert that the company does not hire freelancers. Huh? How would they know?

You want to talk with someone in the department most likely to need your services. Whether you have a source for names (such as a professional association or corporate directory) or are calling around the company for names or exploring the corporate website, it helps to have some idea of how far up the organizational pyramid you must climb to find someone with the authority to engage you.

When you are unsure of whom to talk to, it's best to overshoot. Someone too high up the ladder can pass your name and contact info down. However, those on the bottom rungs fear that any talent they refer will facilitate their own layoff. They would rather be seen as indispensable than offer up the name of their own as-needed replacement. And if they do hand over your info, their endorsement does not lend prestige to your name.

When you call someone who proves not to be a relevant

contact, ask for a name within the company. If they offer to transfer your call, get the person's name and phone number *in case the call gets cut off.* Record this, of course, in your database. Record the name of your initial contact too. When you are transferred, say "John Smith suggested I talk to you," setting it up as a warmer referral.

Work with the company staff skillfully. If you don't have a name, start with the main phone number. Ask for the individual by asking for the title most likely to hire someone for your services. (For me, it's typically director of marketing communications.) Quite possibly the individual answering the main phone number has no idea what you are talking about. Be prepared to discuss your function in very elementary, tangible terms, e.g., "I'm looking for the person in charge of corporate ads and brochures."

If you get nowhere, ask to talk to the administrative assistant to the vice president or director of the function in which you are interested. Write down the name and any contact info you can obtain, as well as the same information for anyone else you talk to.

The initial contact may be able to help you. If so, let them. Don't evade questions and insist on talking only to your intended target. These individuals know the kind of people their department works with. If you get an assignment, you'll be working closely with the administrative assistant on acquiring information, admin details, and getting your invoice transported to the accounting department. Treat these people with respect.

You can have too much of a good thing, which in this case are contacts. You may speak to an underling who brings your name to the boss or to the staff meeting. Perhaps someone higher up also has your name, more than likely because you contacted all involved. If one individual has taken up your case, a second contact may abandon you.

So for best results, cultivate one source in a company at a time (unless contacting departments or functions within a decentralized organization, in which case there may be no, or minimal, interaction between managers).

Watch for this problem when working from a professional directory in which several people from the same department are listed. Start by noting the possible interrelationships of the individuals, looking at job titles, and even observing similarities among area codes and phone numbers to guess who works together. Then choose your champion from the most relevant titles, aiming at someone who appears to have the clout to choose you but, ideally, not so much clout that they are entirely isolated from the tasks you perform.

If you don't hear anything from your preferred contact for three weeks or more, you can assume that no one knows who you are and your first contact has taken no action. In this situation, call someone else from your list.

What if my initial (but wrong) corporate contact asks for more information?

Answer him.

Telephoning is about exchanging honest information. Don't think your sizzle is so sizzling that it will overturn long-standing office practices. *"We've never used a freelancer in the past twenty-five years, but your benefit to the bottom line is so extraordinary that we are making an exception for you. Thank God you called. Is a check for a million dollars enough?"*

Vague, evasive, non-concrete answers do not motivate staff to put you through to the executive pronto so the top dog can get the full story on how the company can enjoy more success than it's ever known. *Au contraire.* They'll recognize your voice and never put you through.

Too many calls and they'll share your name with other staff who cover their phones over lunch. Then their only concern will be keeping the conversation as brief as possible and getting rid of you.

In some instances you may never get the name of a right person to talk to. Doesn't matter. If you are phoning a long list of prospects, one name simply doesn't matter so much. Keep the company in mind and you may discover an "in" someday, perhaps as you are reading a professional journal or talking to an acquaintance at church. Who knows?

How do I get my sales phone call past the gatekeeper?

There's a lot of talk in telephone-sales circles about getting past the gatekeeper. In my experience, gatekeepers are golden. I don't see why you'd want to get past them.

Gatekeepers can tell you who in the company actually uses your type of service and give you the direct phone number. I've actually had administrative assistants do this for me in companies that have super rigid rules in the employee handbook about blocking outside callers.

They can assess your potential contribution to a project and, in effect, make your sales pitch for you. They can present your contact info to their manager as an important resource—or they can dump it right in the trash.

Once you have an assignment, they can be your day-to-day contact, letting you know when the boss will be back from vacation, overnighting background info, and explaining the company's positioning, marketing, and everything else just as effectively (or even better) than anyone else on the project.

And they can help you get your invoice paid promptly. Back when I was a single mother of three and living paycheck to paycheck, on several occasions I called the admin and asked for her help. (In practice, the vast majority were female.) I explained that her company was my most important client this month and now I really am counting on their check to pay my bills by the first of the month. Sympathy for my difficult situation got her out of her chair and talking to her friend in accounting much more effectively than threats about small claims court and collection agencies. (As though Fortune 500 clients are scared.)

As an aside, the admin has probably calculated your annual income by multiplying your hourly rate by forty hours per week for fifty or fifty-two weeks per year. Very unrealistic, we know. You are not obliged to open your books to her, but depending on the flow of the conversation, you may want to free her from a misconception of how much money you have flowing in.

In working with an admin, be friendly and appreciative. The last thing you want is to be dismissive and condescending. After all, our services are all about helping people. When clients buy our services, we're helping everyone on their team, including the administrative assistant.

How do I telephone an impenetrable corporate fortress?

What is the best strategy when the corporate person you're trying to reach with your marketing is extremely insulated? When it appears that your marketing target doesn't open his own mail and allows the administrative assistant to screen (and pass judgment) on everything? When the admin will not put your call through nor give you the intended person's email address?

Here are three ideas on how to proceed.

Number 1. Dress up as the grim reaper and get past the receptionist by telling her you are there to deliver a singing birthday telegram. (I can lend you my outfit but you may find the sleeves a little short.)

Number 2. Send your spouse to pace up and down the front sidewalk of the target company wearing a sandwich-board sign saying you need work.

Number 3. Tie a copy of your letter to a rock and throw it through the window.

The first two have an advantage over the third because they're legal. However, I'm sure they've been done before and are no longer fresh and fun. The third may be the most emotionally satisfying, but don't tell anyone I said that.

Seriously, if you really want to work with that particular person, I'd advise contacting him or her through more than one channel: phone, postal mail, email, etc.

But wait, you've already done that.

I suggest putting this company on the back burner. Remember all of the names you have there in case you ever happen upon someone who could serve as your entrée, but for the time being, end this seemingly hopeless pursuit.

I suspect this is all for the best. This company flashes neon signs of being a miserable client. Inaccessible and egotistical executives, with support staff who share these characteristics. It could be exceedingly difficult to move projects along to completion or obtain needed information. And if your check is late, good luck in finding anyone willing to follow up on it for you.

If you aim to contact a large number of relevant individuals for assignments, as I recommend, this individual represents only a small fraction of your database. Insignificant and not worthy of your concern.

You make calls to offer people your help, not to pester them. Because you choose whom to call with care, they should be pleased to hear from you. Minimally, they should tolerate your approach and consider keeping you on file in case they need you later.

Simply move on to the next name. Take your offer to someone who will value it and who has opened the communication channels to receive it.

When do I call a prospect by their first name?

The short answer is always.

Typically I never think about this until I'm on the phone and the moment to address the individual arises. Then I've been known to panic quietly, second guessing and third guessing myself, unable to decide if an important person should be called Jane/Joe or Ms. Smith/Mr. Smith.

Therefore, I've developed a standard policy and I stick with it. I always address everyone by his or her first name. No exceptions.

There are two problems with addressing those at the pinnacle of the pyramid more formally. The first is determining whom to call by Mr. or Ms. Only the CEO? VPs and above? Everyone in the organization? It's a touchy decision and must be made instantly. Your indecision may leave you stuttering and uncomfortable, causing you to manage the call miserably.

Then there's the second problem: Do you eventually start calling the executive by his or her first name? If so, when do you make the switch?

If the executive never says anything about his/her name, you could be the only individual on the project calling them by their formal name for the rest of the relationship, perhaps even for years.

Use their first name exactly as they do. The list you are calling from may show Charles A. Smith. They answer the phone, "Chuck here." So respond, "Hi, Chuck." Not "Hi, Charles," since they've just told you the name they go by. And certainly not *Mr. Smith*.

This is one reason you have to listen actively as you make phone calls. Do not absentmindedly scroll through your emails until someone gets on the line.

Remember Mary Richards on the old *Mary Tyler Moore Show*? Don't be like Mary! With the exception of her single date with Lou towards the end of the last season, she resolutely called him Mr. Grant. Everyone else, regardless of gender or rank, consistently called him by his first name. Making this even more pathetic was her reputation for having *spunk*!

Of course, this is an American thing. Practices may vary in other cultures.

Should I phone my last employer for assignments?

Let's say you've been laid off from your previous job and want to start telephoning to drum up solopro freelance and consulting projects. Your first thought may be (reasonably, I may add) to call your last employer for assignments. Let's start to analyze this move with a question: Why haven't they already asked you to do some work for them? Obviously they know you are available.

If they haven't called, here's a second question: Did they strew your path with rose petals as you last left the building? If the answer is *yes*, go right ahead and phone them. They may really want you. If the answer is anything less, take them off your phone list . . . forever! Sure, it seems logical to call them first. As a recent insider, you're the best qualified person to do what you've actually done in the past. You know the product, the process, the personalities, and everything else that will help you succeed.

But here's the problem: Your anger and insecurities will serve as mile-wide roadblocks to making the call. You'll see yourself as tremendously scared of phoning when the real problem is your dread of calling only this one person. So take them off your list and you'll remove the most overwhelming impediment to making phone calls and reaching out to prospects. Free yourself to make a fresh start.

Perhaps one day you will run into a former coworker at the grocery. If they ask how you're doing, you may decide to remark casually that you are freelancing *if they ever need some help*. That's it. If they want you, they know where you are. And since you've been let go, they can easily deduce you'd welcome paying work.

They know better than anyone that you have plenty of time available to freelance or consult for them. So move on.

As country singer Randy Travis sings, "Since my phone still ain't ringing, I assume it still ain't you."

How much research should I do before phoning a prospect?

The real research is done in selecting your list, not in conducting comprehensive research on each corporate prospect in order to strategize a simple call.

Evaluate your phone list. If you are working from a high-quality list, you'll have the individual's name, job title, direct phone number, and direct email address. Oh, and not coincidentally, the list will consist of individuals who are highly likely to need your work.

That's all you need to start phoning. If you are curious about the company as a whole, you can indulge in a glance at the website while waiting for your person to answer. Remember that most calls will result only in your leaving a voicemail message. Even if you reach a live person, they won't grant you enough time to show off your exhaustive research on their firm.

If you happen to have a factoid of interest (for instance, that you have worked with the same client as them), slide this into your message in as few words as possible: "I was just looking at your website and I see you use the patented XYZ process, just as I have been doing for years."

Why over-researching is bad. Over-researching is a time waster that prevents you from completing a day's worth of calls. Even worse, it may enable you to feel noble about your hard work while shirking your primary task: phoning.

There's no reason you have to be an expert when prospects pick up the phone on your first contact with them. If they want to talk awhile, start implementing your process.

"Eeek, a process? I need at least a month to roll out my process," you may say.

Not really. Everyone has the same process: collect information, propose plan, finalize plan with client, implement, obtain feedback, tweak, and so it goes. So start the fact-finding process. That's what makes you a true consultant, i.e., a problem solver, rather than a mere worker bee.

Freelancers and consultants who value their time are not embarrassed to start with questions rather than rattling off in-depth research findings or even ground-breaking solutions. Fact finding is a key part of the process, not a pre-assignment giveaway (beyond what is necessary to write a proposal or determine a price).

In other words, start by asking questions, not by answering them. If they want specifics about how you will solve their problem, tell them you need time for preliminary research and analysis. And certainly don't quote a project fee in your first conversation—that's a sure way to underprice.

Expect the prospect's research assistance. It is totally appropriate to ask the prospect to help you conduct research. Request that they email and/or overnight to you anything that will help you understand their company and the problem or assignment at hand. They may provide print publications, internal emails, contact information for in-house experts, competitors' web links, etc.

Don't overthink your preparation for the initial call. Save your analysis for prospects who are interested in hearing it!

What do I offer that no one else offers? What can I do for you that you can't do for yourself?

There are many ways to restate a question you will often be asked: Why should they choose me? What do I do better than the prospect him/herself? How am I better than the competition?

That depends on the service you offer. However, here's an answer that I often use, especially when they ask what I do that they can't do themselves. (It happens all the time in soliciting writing assignments from corporate communications departments.)

I simply say that they may be the best person to write the assignment in question, but that I can prioritize the assignment in a way they cannot. I don't have the administrative and supervisory priorities they face, rarely attend meetings, and simply sit at my desk for hours giving their work my complete attention.

Because I work with them one on one, they can have as much input into the work as they want at every step of the way, from defining the big issues such as target market or tone, to detailed wordsmithing through each draft.

What not to say: that you can do it better than them.

Sure, there may be rare exceptions, such as when a corporate star on the fast track to promotions assumes responsibility for a function he or she has no background in. But generally speaking, position yourself as their partner in accomplishing the work, not as someone who will outshine them.

You may bring a wider perspective to the project, thanks to experience in multiple companies or industries or projects. That's an interesting argument to enlist, but I've never gone in this direction. My experience is that hiring managers most value solopros who support their vision without overly rocking the boat. However, that's because I usually write articles and materials in support of existing marketing platforms. On the other hand, some consultants are brought in specifically to shake things up.

And don't fall into the trap of comparing yourself to the competition. Generally, you don't know the competition. They may say, "I have several people to choose among. Why should I choose you?"

Dang if I know, you may be thinking. If you don't know the competition, you can't know why you are better. If you do know the competition, it puts you in a bad light to badmouth them.

You may decide to say something like, "I am unable to evaluate others. All I can say is that I am very skilled at [name the talent] and I'm confident I can do a great job for you."

How do I answer difficult questions?

The truth is a good starting place for coming up with an answer. When you're not sure what to say, experiment with the truth. Why not? Aren't you offering a valuable service at a fair price? There's nothing there you need to disguise. If there is something inadequate about your service or your work habits, remedy the problem rather than looking for a clever way to disguise it.

Here is a question I find uncomfortable, with a possible

answer. Maybe you can come up with a better answer that is more true for you.

Why do you charge so much? I can find foreign workers who charge much less. Answer: I stand by my work and stay with it until you are satisfied. I have had many happy customers and I know I can complete this assignment successfully. My prices are typical of this market. (Note: With an answer like this, make sure the work arrangement you offer is priced adequately. Don't promise unlimited revisions at bargain-basement prices.)

What question do you most dread? Ask yourself that question before someone else does. I invite you to post it to my blog so I and other readers can take a stab at it. Visit *http://budurl.com/plspost* and enter your question as a comment.

How many phone calls does it take to start getting solopro freelance or consulting assignments?

My system for how to start making money quickly as a freelancer or consultant calls for telephoning the corporate managers most likely to need (and pay for) your services.

The secret (with *secret* here meaning *how it works*) is to call large numbers of people, all of them valid prospects for what you offer.

And my large number of choice is 1,000 individuals.

Yes, you read that right. 1,000!

And the secret of calling 1,000 prospects? (Again, *secret* means *how it works*.) Well, the secret is to break the task down into achievable parts.

You only need to make fifty calls a day. Then do that five work days a week for four weeks. At the end of four weeks you will have made 1,000 calls.

Be honest, what did you think when you read the 1,000 number? The first time I read it (in *The Well-Fed Writer* by Peter Bowerman), I thought, *Well, sure, if you call 1,000 people, you ought to get at least one assignment.*

And then I thought about what I thought, and I thought, *Wow, this will work. This is something I can control and that will get results!*

I am making the world a better place one call at a time, fifty calls a day. I had already been phoning when I saw the number in print. Previously, I believed that three calls every day were enough. I believed that somehow the universe would be less annoyed with me if I restricted how many times I bothered others on any given day. But upon reflection, each of those last forty-seven calls is as valid as the first three. Since I only phone people whom I believe can benefit from my services, I am offering my help to more people every day, which is all for the good.

What's it like in practice to make 1,000 calls in a single month? Well, I still don't know. Every time work has slowed down for some reason (such as working a full-time corporate job for a few years), I've resumed marketing and have filled my plate with assignments way before I have completed 1,000. At that point I've pulled back to substantially fewer calls per day to free up time for paying work.

This number may not be right for you. You may not have a good calling list so it will take substantial time to find good names and their contact info every day. You may be heavily involved in the quest for a full-time job. You may still be warming up to telephoning and find fifty calls way too stressful. The rest of your life (e.g., family obligations) may be interfering.

Motivated or desperate. The 1,000 number is for those who are highly motivated to earn money quickly. Alternatively, it is for those who are desperate. (The two situations can be pretty similar in real life.) Either way, it is a course of intense action to obtain paying results soon.

If fifty calls per day aren't for you, determine your own number. Telephoning is not an all-or-nothing practice. But the more calls you make, the faster you get work.

Even one call is better than none. God is calling, *so buy a lottery ticket already.*

The very first call is the most important one of all. That's one small step to your first client, one giant leap to building a successful practice.

What percentage of prospecting phone calls is successful?

Let's start with actual numbers on the responses (that is, people who are interested, not necessarily people who give an assignment at this time): **5% is tremendous, 2% is excellent, and 1% is acceptable.**

Now for some background if you enjoy this sort of thing. (Many people don't.)

Since I recommend making large numbers of phone calls to generate freelance and consulting assignments, I am often asked how many calls should be made to obtain a certain number of sales conversations or even assignments.

This is difficult to determine.

For starters, there are so many variables that you are comparing apples to orange golf balls. Variables include your specialty, the quality of your approach (e.g., how experienced you are on the phone, how persuasive your email is), your ability to convert the prospect to an actual customer, the quality and relevance of the calling list you have developed, any special links to the people called (such as belonging to the same professional organization as you), etc.

I confess: it may take a lot of telephone calls to succeed. But I'd love to see how solid figures for other marketing efforts measure up. (It appears that very few practitioners of other prospecting techniques track their results and develop valid data.)

If you feel your response is too low, test another marketing channel to compare results. Record hard data so you have something to analyze.

Try live networking events. Count up the total number of people you talk with and the number of positive, let's-move-forward-at-least-in-a-small-way responses you gather.

Or track your social media results. Friends have told me that it takes years to get business through social media such as Facebook, LinkedIn, and Twitter. They have also told me that they know someone else (not themselves!) who actually did get a paying client through this channel. Big deal!

How do I know if my phone campaign is working?

A reader of my blog asked if based on call results, how you know you're either working with the wrong list or giving the wrong pitch:

I've just started using your methods and have done only twenty calls. I left about nineteen voicemails. I don't know how many will call back. If I get one callback, or none, or a bunch—what does that tell me? Should I modify the pitch? Are one hundred calls enough to know?

Why it takes time to get results. We would like to think that potential hirers are sitting at their desks shuffling papers until we call. When we suggest our services, they spring to action, relieved to find the answer to their prayers. So of course, they take our call. Unless they are not at their desk. In which case they call immediately after their 3 P.M. run to Starbucks.

Believe it or not, the people we call do not have returning our call as their top priority. A few are curious and will call back immediately. Some are interested, but having no need now, they file our names away without getting back to us. Some are out of the office for two weeks and won't pick up our message until next week. Some may refer us to others who need our services without letting us know. (Yes, it has happened to me. One person I was referred to called about a year and a half later.)

The first days of phoning are the most frustrating. You mostly talk to voicemail and no one calls back. Several days into the process, you start to get a few callbacks, soothing your fears that your calls are not landing with anyone at all.

So it takes days or even weeks to get positive responses, regardless of how many calls you make on day one. At the beginning you may suspect that the technology is on the fritz because even though you hear the voicemail clicking on at the other end, it seems as if you are connecting with no one. As the days pass and you continue to phone, the number of responses will grow due to the cumulative impact of all that effort. Hang in there—you knew in advance it may take a month of plowing to reap successes.

Here's the question you should ask yourself: What else would I do with my time to get work if I were not making these phone calls? If you have something more effective in mind, take a break from phoning and try it out. Or are you considering any of the following...?

Giving up on freelancing/consulting and getting a real job? If you hate marketing of every sort, this may be just right for you. Face it. Freelancing and consulting will require con-

sistent marketing until you die. Or until you retire. Which-
ever comes first.

But what if you are trying to solopro because you can't get
a job? Giving up on freelancing/consulting doesn't automatically solve your employment problem. Instead, if you want a
regular job, keep applying while you phone for solopro work.
There's no conflict between the two.

**Networking, either in person or online through Twit-
ter, Facebook, LinkedIn, etc.?** I assume that if you have
started on any of these or similar services, you've already
used these channels to publicize your freelancing/consulting.
Maybe not for hours every day, but you have emailed family
and friends and posted update notes to your online profiles,
haven't you?

These channels are built on know, like, and trust. They'll
take much longer than thirty days to generate income, most
likely. And if you are going to switch over totally to these
channels, what are you going to do strategically to convert
social connections into paying assignments?

Watching TV? Many people have taken this route. I confess, I've done it too.

My favorite diversion was *America's Next Top Model* mara-
thons. Now it's *Project Runway*. What's yours?

The days will pass whether you phone or not. If you don't
have a more effective marketing technique, stay with the
phoning.

Now let's back up to the original question: How do you
know you're either working with the wrong list or giving the
wrong pitch?

You know if you are working with the wrong list or giving the wrong pitch because you are going after assignments
similar to your last good job. You don't have to talk to pros-

pects to determine their needs because you have spent years toiling in their industries and in their functional areas so you already know their needs.

You already know what they need and how they perceive their problems and what keeps them up at night. Sit back and remember what your boss used to complain about over coffee. What he or she requested more of during performance reviews and annual objective-writing sessions.

The voicemail messages you leave and to which no one has responded teach you nothing. Unless you are a mind reader.

There are a few people who will talk to you but do not need your services. Because their number is small and because they have talked to you, it is very possible to put too much credence in what they tell you and overly rely on it. And since their answer contains a *no* or at least a *not now*, it is easy to become unreasonably discouraged.

They may say they don't need you because they do the work themselves. Or they laid people off so why would they hire a freelancer? Or they have no business coming in. Or they can't spend the money.

However, the next person you phone may hire you because they are too busy doing the work themselves. Or they need a freelancer because they had to let their employees go. Or they want to expand their marketing, product development, etc. to generate more business. Or they have to spend the money because they are stuck and have an intense need for your services. Or they have the money because they've laid off full-time workers.

You will get assignments, or at least questions about services prospects may need, if you are persistent. This is the input that most helps you shape future marketing.

I know . . . kind of frustrating that you don't get the input you need until you get assignments that somewhat relieve the intensity of your questions. That's life.

How can I cope with rejection?

Wait until you actually experience it to deal with it. I myself never experience true rejection. Rejection is something very personal. It's when people strike at the core of who you are and cast you aside.

Define it this way and you may never be rejected. People don't use freelancers or consultants or they don't return calls or they don't even check their voicemail or they already have people they use. The resulting *no* is not rejection, just reality.

Remember that people lie. If you subscribe to lots of marketing emails as I do, you'll see that others in your profession or industry are supposedly making fortunes and have the lives of their dreams. Maybe yes, maybe no. There's no way to know.

But this I do know: people love to tell their happy stories, not talk about all the toil that has not yet paid off. If you repeatedly meet with others in your business, over time you may hear them tell the same story more than once, generally about a serendipitous, even cute, meet-up that resulted in work. You can be fairly certain that most work—if indeed, the individual has a respectable workload—did not come via *cute*.

Every technique to build business involves contacting many more people than those who say yes.

But here's the main way to deal with anyone who actually *rejects* you: simply erase from your calling list anyone who gives you bad vibes. Erase them figuratively, not literally. You want to keep their name on file, complete with comments on what they said, so you don't accidentally call them again.

Go on to the other 999 names. Next!

There's absolutely no reason to set yourself up for a second round of negativity. Even if they are later interested in your services, you wouldn't want to work with them, would you? Fortunately, when you are self-employed, no one can make you.

Aren't you glad you know up-front what they're like? This is a wonderful opportunity to save yourself from months of aggravation.

Are my phone calls a nuisance?

Your services benefit users who choose to avail themselves of your work. They have been individually selected to receive your call.

They should be pleased to hear from you. (I mean this with 100% of my heart!)

And if they tell you they want no further calls, you note this and never call again.

So, no, your calls are not a nuisance.

Do you feel the love?

Granted, the love isn't constant. But there's a surprising experience of acceptance out there!

The predominant response to phone calls is absolutely nothing. The vast majority of calls go to voicemail and no one calls back, or at least not right away.

An infinitesimally small number are answered by a live human and dispatched quickly and rudely.

A modest number of the people you reach are actively in the market for your services and currently have a need or foresee using your services in the near future.

And some have no near-term need but are warm and encouraging. Some have been self-employed professionals offering the services you offer but are now in corporate employment. They enjoy talking about what made their business a success, how they faced key challenges, and may even give leads to companies that used their services.

A few people for whom you leave messages will call back simply to tell you pleasantly they have no needs. These exchanges seem brief and benign, but don't instantly discount them because no work is forthcoming. Interpret this as a pat on the back when people who could simply delete the message go to the effort to respond.

Some people will welcome your call, recognizing that you are doing what they should be doing. This is especially true for other small-business people that are not doing as much marketing as they need to do.

Finally, there are the corporate contacts who may eagerly anticipate—or fearfully dread—going the solopro path in the future. There's no way of knowing how many of these people entertain our calls and ask for our marketing links and materials to file in case they need inspiration for their own businesses down the line. But given the pace of corporate layoffs, I suspect their numbers are substantial.

Yes, there is some love out there. Recognize and cherish it.

What if everyone telephoned to find solopro assignments?

While reading this book, I'd guess you have thought, *hmm*, sounds like targeted phoning may work, but what if everyone did it? Just as HR departments are deluged with unread résumés, managers will soon delete all solopros' voicemails as soon as they recognize them as marketing.

Won't happen.

Well, that deletion thing may happen. There are always people who prove to themselves how important they are by treating other people like crap.

Now back to the question itself. Everyone (the group that includes all freelancers and all consultants) will never telephone a long list of people for assignments.

Many people have never made such a phone call and never will. Others make a handful and quit. *Thank God it doesn't work*, they think. *I tried a call or two and I proved it doesn't work!*

For those who go on to make tens or even hundreds of calls, are they creating a nuisance that should inspire federal legislation to end corporate telemarketing? Not if callers are doing it my way. I want people to offer a service in which they are experts, to call only the best prospects for these services, and to make these calls themselves.

When you do it my way, it's impossible to be spammy. Phoning is work and you don't want to waste your effort. You evaluate each name as you call and don't plow through long, irrelevant lists if you don't believe the calls will pay off. In short, you pay attention and save yourself from useless work.

And if everyone phoned company managers to obtain solopro assignments, all I can say is: *What a wonderful world that would be if we all offered our talents directly to the people who could benefit from them.*

If adults quit hiding behind their mother's skirts (or nowadays, emails) and told the right people what they could do to help without the I-just-want-to-be-your-friend ambiguity of social media, it would be all for the best.

Each of us has a contribution to make. Let us offer our unique contributions to the world with pride in our talents.

To the point:

- Any type of marketing requires lots of actions to be effective. The law of large numbers is a law because it has been proven again and again.

- Plan to make many calls in your first month. I suggest aiming for 1,000 calls. Yes, it can be done. However, in practice, you'll probably land assignments long before you complete that many calls and then slow down your phoning pace so you can complete paying work.

- A simple script, presented conversationally, works best. Don't look for "can't fail" power phrases and questions.

- You will frequently hear the word "no." Get used to it. True rejection stings and is exceedingly rare. You may never experience rejection.

- Remember that phoning the right people to offer the help they need makes the world a better place, one call at a time.

Step 5

Price, Bill, and Collect for Success

Most of us go solopro to make some money. This chapter is about the money side of the work. So here's the info you've been waiting for.

Or have you?

Many people don't want to phone prospects, but in practice they detest dealing with pricing, invoicing, and collecting even more.

Especially collecting.

Even more so, collecting when the check doesn't simply show up in the mail and they have to get somewhat *emphatic*, shall we say.

Managing the money aspect separates the men from the boys, the careerists from the hobbyists, and the adults from the children.

What is the first task each day for a solopro?

Every day, your first task is to determine if you should invoice a client. If you should, do so!

Never postpone invoicing more than twenty-four hours from the event that triggers it. (Be honest though. A project isn't *final* until the client agrees that it's done—unless your agreement in the beginning defines completion differently. Just because you really need the money doesn't transform the first go-round into the final product.) The fresher the project is in your mind, the easier it is to prepare an accurate invoice. And the sooner you invoice, the sooner you get paid.

Good clients expect to pay. Prompt, accurate invoicing is just as central to superior customer service as is delivering the completed assignment by deadline.

How should I charge and how much should I charge?

Ah, the critical questions. Issues you will revisit again and again.

Difficult as it is to come up with a figure, you have to choose a number right from the start. In certain instances it may be appropriate to ask the client what the typical pay is—writing an article for a longstanding magazine is that type of situation—but generally speaking, you need to know your rate. Don't pass the task of determining this to the prospect.

Read on to learn more about the three ways of determining your rate.

Charge by the hour. A straight cost-per-hour quote compensates you fairly for your time but presents other problems, including the flip sides of the arguments for other pricing schemes below. In particular, as you gain speed over time on recurring projects, your total fee decreases if there are no adjustments to the hourly rate. Also, some argue that hourly billing commoditizes your services.

Charge by the project. The second is the flat rate. Some believe this is the way to go to avoid allowing the client to measure and challenge your hours and to prevent sticker shock since freelance and consulting hourly rates are much higher than the hourly rates for salaried employees.

You know up front how much you will earn. The client knows exactly what the cost will be and can budget for it. The downside is that you cannot be certain how much time the project will require. The first assignment for a client may entail a steep learning curve, but you may decide to absorb some of this time in the hope of more assignments in the future.

Later assignments will take less time. Since you are quoting by the project, the time saved need not be revealed to the client. After all, just because you get faster and better at doing recurring assignments does not mean you should be paid less for the same result.

In addition to not knowing how much time you will need at your end for the first assignment from a client, you don't know the work patterns of the client. There is no way of knowing how many reviews and revisions a client will demand, how many staffers present conflicting input, how difficult it will be to collect the information you need, etc. This problem can be mitigated with a contract that pins down how many revisions you'll do and other dimensions of the project.

When charging by the project, pad your time estimate because everything takes longer than you think it will. The experts say by 10%, but if the customer has lots of cooks in the kitchen, 25% or even more may be appropriate. You can never know what additional requests your client will make or how many times they may change their minds, and yes, it is perfectly fair to charge for all this. You'll also be more benign in handling their indecision and other flaws if you are getting paid for the extra demands their internal politics or individual dithering places on you.

Be sure to define the project in your contract or email of understanding. If not, you may be subject to endless revisions and countless meandering phone calls. Also, define how you know when the project is completed. At the end of a project, clients may be in a rush and determine that they can tweak it on their own without you. The project goes out their door or is indefinitely postponed and they never get back to you to pay. Let them know that if you don't hear from them within two weeks, or another specified time period, at any phase of the cycle, the project will be deemed completed and you will invoice at that time. (Record the submission date as your initial date for measuring this period. That's a good reason to repeat by phone that you have sent work via email.)

Warning: never reveal your estimate for a project during the initial phone call. You'll always underestimate it. Give yourself at least twenty-four hours to work with the numbers and sleep on it.

Charge by the value. The third way is by value of the work completed. For instance, if your work may result in $50,000 in sales and your value is determined as 10% of the total, your fee would be $5,000.

I have never used the value system. It's sort of like being paid a commission because value is based on results. However, unlike a commission, you are paid whether anticipated results occur or not. I find it unappealing to accept something similar to a commission when I accept no risk on the project. In addition, how would I determine and verify total sales or other results if the client is not forthcoming?

However, many outstanding solopros swear by this arrangement. Certain situations may legitimately require special pricing arrangements. For instance, some direct-mail copywriting assignments pay royalties based on sales.

Please note: I do not base my price on value, but I am quite comfortable charging a substantial hourly or project rate for my work. Yes, my work has "value," and I price accordingly. However, that's not my criterion in pricing in the same way that I understand other freelancers and consultants to practice value pricing.

My magic formula for hourly rates

If you are offering a solopro service similar to the work you did on your last good job, your salary reflected your market value. Here is a way to convert that value into a freelance rate. This is my ordained pricing formula for hourly rates. Cue lightning bolt. Read in your best Charlton Heston voice . . . and then feel free to adapt this advice as you wish.

First, take your annual salary at your last good corporate job and divide it by 1,000. (For those of us who are not mathematically inclined, delete the comma and the last three numbers.) If your salary was $50,000, this number would be 50. If your salary was $100,000, the number would be 100.

Desired hourly rate: Annual salary divided by 1,000, multiplied by 2. This is roughly similar to four times your salaried hourly rate.

Example: $50,000 per year salary, $100 hourly rate.

Pretty good hourly rate: Annual salary divided by 1,000. This is roughly similar to two times your salaried hourly rate.

Example: $50,000 per year salary, $50 hourly rate.

Rock-bottom rate for special circumstances: For example, this type of work is entirely new to you and you want the learning experience. $25 per hour. (This is, admittedly, an arbitrary number I have invented.)

Anything below this rate is totally and always unacceptable. Late at night you may be paging through some online job bank and thinking that anything is better than nothing. Not true: something is not always better than nothing because it claims your time. Therefore, you can't make phone calls or do other marketing in support of your business. Not taking low-paying assignments allows you free time to land better-paying work.

Novices to freelancing/consulting often experience sticker shock when searching the Internet for pricing schedules or when working with the formulas I have presented. My recommendations result in hourly rates far in excess of what you probably earned on payroll.

While you felt acclimated and comfortable at your last job, you may be undertaking your first entrepreneurial effort with trepidation or downright fear. So how can you expect *more* pay?

You multiply the hourly rate I have suggested by forty hours a week and then multiply by fifty weeks a year. (The nice round numbers make it easy to calculate in your head and *generously* allow two weeks of vacation, though you may hope you will be too busy to think about a vacation.) The number seems astronomical. *Why not simply set the rate more competitively and postpone buying the yacht?* you ask.

Let's talk about competition and market rates

It's mathematically impossible to underprice competitors. Here's why:

Some people actually believe the way to win clients is to offer their services for free at the beginning to prove their value and assemble a portfolio. *Oy vey!* The only way to underprice these people is for you to pay the client. Frankly, I'd bet some people actually would pay big-name prospects for the prestige it would lend their portfolio and client list.

Anyway, I don't think this works, though I've never tried it, I'm pleased to say. Charities may accept free work, but for-profit organizations would (and should!) not feel comfortable with such an arrangement. They would (and should!) suspect the individual is too naïve and amateurish to deliver a good product, and thus a waste of their time.

(Well . . . at least I'd like to think companies would reject free work. A lot of them are using free interns who have already graduated from college, and they are using them for extended periods of time. So who knows what work, if any, is too sophisticated for them to accept for free?)

Some solopros search the Internet, websites of professional organizations, archives of online forums, and other resources to determine the market rate. However, while there may be some small niche in which there is a *market rate*, for most specialties the market is vast.

Because of the Internet and other electronic communications, the marketplace is international. If your field does not legally require a very specific credential, people are entering with a variety of educational and experiential backgrounds. It's impossible to delineate clearly who the competition is. Is it the New York specialists in prestige firms? The no-confidence newbie happy to earn $10 an hour? The people vying for rock-bottom wages on guru.com, elance.com, and similar services?

Prospective clients may be eager to tell you your fee is too high, but it's the rare prospect who will tell you your price is too low. They may say something like, "That sounds in the ballpark," but are you really in the ballpark or is your price too low?

Then there's the issue of experience. I once wanted to explore a new niche. I sent out an email to firms that might offer work and suggested the rock-bottom rate of $25 per hour on my first assignments, explaining my strengths and weaknesses and admitting that I would need hands-on guidance as a novice. I got some takers, and it was a fair deal for all.

Actually I did this twice with two different specialties that called for writing skills. In both instances I decided that the new career directions would pay off both financially and in terms of personal satisfaction only if I immersed myself in them, learned a lot, and built up a professional network. I chose to stay with my current work rather than branch out into other fields. In other words, I got these fantasies out of my system and made a few bucks in the process instead of paying for credentials before experiencing the work.

There is no way to be sure you have priced right because each client is different. Some pros ask what the budget is before naming their price. This may come off as cagey and manipulative—can't help wondering if they ever come in with a figure that does not include all available funds—but many people out there recommend this and claim to do it themselves.

If you feel comfortable doing this, it may yield useful information. One graceful explanation is that you want to tailor a proposal within their means.

Remember that being turned down for an assignment because you've asked for too much money is not the worst thing that can happen to you. The worst thing that can happen is to agree to do too much work for way too little money. You're too busy to take on the next assignment that comes along or even campaign for more work, and while you may be pleased initially simply to be working, you'll soon seethe as you toil to meet deadlines.

What do I say when clients ask my hourly rate?

It's best to initiate a conversation about the project and how well you can handle it. Ask questions such as, *What are you trying to achieve?* Or simply, *What do you have in mind?* Unless you are positioning yourself as the lowest-cost provider—and I certainly don't recommend that!—you don't especially want to blurt out your hourly rate.

Another conversational tack: *I prefer to work out a project fee so that you can have confidence in budgeting for the project.* Or:

I'm sure we can work out a mutually acceptable fee arrangement, especially if this is your first conversation with them and no specific project is on the table.

But what if they act like you're beating around the bush and demand a specific number? Give them your number! (You're not ashamed of it, are you?) Then follow up with a statement such as: *How does that sound to you?* Or: *Is this about what you were expecting?*

Then shut up and let them speak.

They may say this is in the ballpark. This means either that they agree with your rate or that you charge less than others. You may never know which. They may say this is on the high side but it may be possible. (Music to my ears, though this may simply be a negotiating tactic.)

They may be indignant. They have a stable of pack mules (er, I mean people) who work at much lower rates than you.

Next! No, I am not suggesting you rudely hang up on them. But it's unlikely you can win over people like this. Just ask if they'd like you to email information to them in case they are interested in your services at some future date.

You've got to wonder about contacts who find people to work so cheaply for them. One possibility is that they are content with low-paid labor even if they have to spend a lot of their own time correcting the work. It's their loss. Another is that they've found workers who do excellent work but don't understand their own value. There will always be people like this. There's nothing to do about this, but you *are* phoning forty-nine other people today, aren't you?

Don't waste time doubting your pay rate, your value as a human being, or your eventual success. Just keep working your way down the list.

How firm should I be on demanding market rate?

There's an entirely different method of determining your rate: simply agree to or reject their offer. This is typically used in organizations that use freelancers/consultants in a structured way. For instance, magazines offer a set rate for articles. In some instances you may be able to negotiate, but you may just have to make a yes or no decision.

In any case, do what is right for you. Everyone is different in levels of experience, confidence, monetary needs, time availability, etc. I've seen people throw away opportunities that would be perfect for them because they hear voices in their head that they are somehow degrading their profession by not demanding rates that they themselves cannot access at this time but others are happily collecting, thank you. So they have no work and no prospects when they could be working on something that would be just right for them. (You'll see this, in particular, with inexperienced solopros fielding requests from nonprofits, educational institutions, and one-person businesses.) Note: I'm not talking about $2 per hour work from the Internet. I'm talking about reasonable but lower offers, usually with a local organization.

For instance, a local freelance writer was substitute teaching for a public school when the principal asked her to write for the school at the same rate she got for subbing. She refused because fellow members of the professional writing association to which she belonged recommended much higher fees. However, this arrangement, in practice, would have been just fine for her.

As I said before, most endeavors don't have a narrowly defined market rate so don't get hung up on what the market is charging. The right fee for you and this specific prospect is solely between you and the client.

What is the right rate to charge in New York City . . . or Chicago . . . or Helena, Montana?

If you solely work off-site and communicate by phone or email, local rates are irrelevant. If your work potentially has a national or international clientele and is transferred electronically, local rates don't matter and may not even exist. Your cost of living is irrelevant to the client, right?

This points out why it is advisable to live somewhere with a low cost of living. (Sometimes that is easier said than done.) Or, if you live somewhere more expensive, you should consider how to make that a competitive advantage. It may mean that you can network easily with industry leaders, or work on-site for major clients, or have access to seminars, libraries, and other important information resources, or attend national professional conferences inexpensively while spending nights in your own bed, or arrange speaking engagements to publicize your work in front of large, important audiences. You may wish to focus on types of work that can only be done up close.

What freelance and consulting clients look for and why it isn't price

Many prospects are not as price conscious as you may assume. Timeliness and excellence may be far more important to them.

People with full-time corporate jobs tend to be very busy. Their days (and evenings) are packed with meetings, preparing for meetings, following up after meetings, firefighting, ad hoc requests from executives, supervising others, goal setting, planning, personnel issues, networking, giving feedback, professional activities, training, Friday happy hour, and a million and one other activities that steal time from producing work. Not only can I devote the majority of daytime work hours to their project, but I can work with them in various ways that allow them as much or as little input as they desire.

If they prefer, they can tell me their thoughts so that it almost seems like dictation—though I put a great deal more thought into it than merely transcribing their words. Then they are free to wordsmith as much as they want. Others want minimal participation, giving me the name of a coworker who will provide direction or asking me to supply subject and treatment ideas.

Any way it happens, it's less work for them.

From their perspective, though, there is a catch to working with someone not on payroll: the client has less control over the day-to-day process. When the person doing the work is a full-time employee, the boss can stop by the underling's desk to see how work is progressing. They can set up mini-meetings along the way to discuss details. They have a say over how it is done, not just the final result.

Quite the contrary with a solopro working offsite. Generally there is a tight deadline and the hired individual is not heard from until that date, when the final deadline is imminent. Sometimes there are meetings or deadlines along the way for corporate input or clarification, but working with a freelancer or consultant is still far less hands-on than doing it all in-house.

Further complicating the challenge is that an outsider is obviously less aware of the corporate culture, company expectations, work flow, products, and anything else you can name. The skilled freelancer or consultant streamlines communications to clarify the assignment without burdening the corporate contact and proceeds with confidence, whether real or faked.

Companies are trusting people they hardly know. So it is more important than ever for them to hire the best. The best freelancers and consultants are extremely competent. They offer a background in the industry in question and the skills to work independently on a project and for a company to which they are completely fresh.

Yes, it is depressing to see the low rates on some online job boards and the low-price providers advertising on Craigslist. But these people do not have inroads on the best corporate assignments. Executives and directors cannot risk their own job performance on unknown people who lack relevant experience.

Too low a price can be perceived as a problem: lack of confidence, lack of competence, or lack of familiarity with corporate processes and expectations, including typical rates of pay.

If the hirer has to re-do the whole project against a tight deadline—or worse yet, do it from scratch because the freelancer falls down on the job, the assignor may have to do just as much work as he would have on his own—with the added stress of an even shorter timeframe.

Your solopro rates: How do you value yourself?

When we equate our salary or our freelance/consulting fees with our self-esteem, we're mucking around in quicksand that can quickly engulf us.

Our fees have nothing to do with our worth as individuals.

Jay Abraham is a famous guy on the Internet who (last I heard) charges $50,000 a day for his counsel. I know, you're asking what he does because that's a business we all want to get in on. I listened to part of one of his free teleseminars and apparently he makes deals.

Is he worth $50,000? If people pay it, then he is worth it. That's his price in the marketplace. Does that mean that if there's another Hurricane Katrina in Jay's neck of the woods that he should be first on the lifeboat? I say *no*. There is no way to assign a dollar value to people's lives.

What we choose to charge should be our calculation of the market value of our services, not a measure of our self-esteem.

It's just money.

Why are starting-out fees as a solopro not as crucial as others may think?

The biggest roadblock to getting started as a freelancer or consultant is deciding what to charge. If you charge too much, potential customers will walk away. If you don't charge enough, you are leaving money on the table. Obviously, not good.

Not only that, but if you don't charge enough, customers may still walk away, figuring that you aren't very good. Or that you are inexperienced and not in touch with the marketplace.

So you fret and worry. Are you charging as much as the market will bear? Are you charging so much that you lose desirable projects? How do you know if you have charged as much as you can?

You want the client to say *yes* when you present your price. Or truly, you want the client to say *yes*, but to wince. And how do you know if the wince is real or if it is to prevent you from raising the price later because you think you are at the brink?

Just thinking about this is enough to give you a headache.

And when you are writing an actual proposal, it's enough to add upset stomach to your health woes.

Now that I've set the stage, here is the number one reason that what you charge is not all that important: Each client stands apart. No one knows what any other client of yours has paid so you are not setting a precedent in pricing jobs for future clients. I assume you have not publicly posted rates on your website or elsewhere!

Granted, there is still the sticky issue of how to raise the price on existing clients. But if you are starting out, existing clients are by definition but a fraction of your future customer base. Furthermore, there are ways to address this issue later on when it becomes a problem.

Your pricing headache will soon start throbbing if you worry years in advance. Today's challenge is snaring your first few assignments. No new client has ever asked me what I was paid for past assignments. Nor has anyone ever asked me for contacts at past client firms so they could verify what I was paid.

No one has ever asked me. And if they did, I wouldn't tell them. Ah, now I remember once again why I freelance and consult. A primary objective of freelancing and consulting should be to have enough different clients that you never feel as powerless as when you wed yourself to a single full-time job and forsake all others.

Each freelance or consulting client is a new day, a fresh start. This makes each proposal you prepare much less of a life-altering event.

I'd like to end this section with a funny story from Tim Ferriss, author of *The 4-Hour Workweek*. There's much in that book that I don't believe would work for most people, starting with the fundamental premise that we can make all the money we need to live a pleasure-filled lifestyle by working only four hours a week. Yet some of his ideas are intriguing…

Ferriss recommends approaching local offices of big-name companies and offering them your services in a small way. For instance, call the area service office of IBM and propose a brown-bag luncheon program on time management. No matter how little you are paid (or even if you do it for free) and no matter how few people show up, he says you can legitimately claim forever after that you have consulted with IBM.

Food for thought. And frankly, I got a good laugh out of it.

It doesn't quite fit my ethics, but it illustrates how in the right circumstances, it may be worthwhile to take a low-paying assignment.

A counteroffer to consider when negotiating your fee

In tough times, prospects may offer to hire you for freelance or consulting work but only at a rate below your usual price, claiming they can't afford to pay market rate.

The experts out there say never to accept a lower hourly fee after you present a figure because you are devaluing your own work. They recommend not cutting a flat project fee without eliminating some aspect of the work. Not only does this preserve the message that your price is consistent with the value you offer and not a mere whim, but it frees up your time to find higher-paying work.

Still, lowering your price is a temptation when work is slow and you are just starting to solopro. And since there is no union or industry-wide price setting, we are each free to do as we wish.

Here's an alternate offer: Suggest working for a lower fee but require full payment upfront. After all, because the sum at risk is low relative to the work time required, there is less downside to you if they walk up front.

And since the prospect's argument for a lower price is essentially that they can't (or won't) pay full rates, they may be telling you they are a poor credit risk (or moral risk). The financial challenges they admit to should warn you that they may be unable to pay promptly when the project is completed. It is always advantageous to structure payment so you receive as large a share as possible as soon as possible, but this is especially true in a yellow-light (caution!) scenario.

Here's another way to handle a too-low offer: postpone. Simply say that you have other opportunities in development that you must follow up on before you would consider their rate. And remind them of the unique benefits you offer. Or even that you are working with other clients now and it wouldn't be fair to accept a lower rate from this prospect. Then get busy and make even more phone calls.

It's tempting to tell off someone who thinks he can get a lower price elsewhere, but in an era of widespread outsourcing and online freelancer databases, it may be possible for them to find someone who is competent yet willing to work for less.

This way the too-low possibility eases your stress in the ongoing phoning phase and gives you confidence in talking to other prospects. If you are new to this business and have had few or even no clients to date, there's no reason to burn bridges.

Take their offer as a good omen and try to better it with the next prospect.

How much should I charge family and friends for my services?

Setting your professional rates is difficult, but here's something even more difficult: determining how much to charge family and friends for your services.

Here's one good option: $0.

Yes, you read that right. Zip.

Let's look at the fundamental issue of helping family and friends on the cheap. It's a perfectly good hobby. It hones your skills, builds confidence, provides intellectual stimulation, and yes, helps others.

If you want to help others, I suggest it may be good to do it for free since even as little as $50 or $100 can mislead you into thinking you have found a specialty that will support you financially. But I assure you, that's not enough money for the work done, unless it is a very small assignment.

You may think that a small amount is enough because you will do less work or give the work lower priority to make the deal financially reasonable.

When people pay anything at all, they expect prompt, letter-perfect service. My résumé clients, for instance, would not be comfortable receiving their final résumés three weeks after the position they want has closed simply because they get a good price. (Furthermore, $100, or even $50, seems like a fortune to the unemployed person writing the check.)

People who pay nothing at all still expect prompt, letter-perfect service. Don't volunteer unless you are willing to put forth your best effort for no pay. Clients shape their opinions of your work based on how you perform, even if you warn them you are cutting corners. If someday in the future they have an opportunity to send someone else your way, they won't recommend you if they don't think much of your work.

Anything less than your best may come back to haunt you (or you may never know that your third cousin twice removed *forgot* to refer you to his boss). And any fee over $0 may prove awkward to collect.

One answer is to redefine upfront the service you offer free so it is not even almost mistaken for the whole enchilada.

Take the résumé example again. I may offer to critique a friend's résumé and make suggestions without applying fingers to keyboard. Critiquing is easy—but creating a final, perfect résumé is more work than I'll do for free.

The favors you do for friends and relatives will set their

opinion of you in concrete for all eternity. "She's not very creative," or "He's not accurate—you've got to review everything he does," they'll say behind your back.

Help them think the best of you. And help them recommend you to their family and friends.

Should I accept assignments on spec?

Sometimes you may be asked to work on spec, that is, speculation as to whether or not the client will accept it and pay for it. When you spell it out, you get a better sense of why it's no good. Assume you will not get the assignment, you will not get paid, and you will not even get meaningful feedback on your work and why it was rejected.

My limited experience working on spec has been exceptionally unsatisfactory. I never got feedback—positive or negative—on the work I did. It was not a learning experience. Also, I had no way of knowing if it was used in full or was tweaked and used in part.

Certainly don't count on the money until it is in your pocket.

What's my inventory?

Yes, you read that right. Solopro service providers have inventory, and that inventory consists of *time*. The passage of time inevitably wipes out our inventory if we are not applying it to paying assignments.

To truly understand this concept, we must think of the work period as having a finite end. If we are measuring by the day, that day ends at midnight. If by the week or month, again, the endpoint is clear. The year ends at midnight on December 31. There's nothing we can do to change that.

Our income goals must be defined within a specific time period. As that period transpires, time is lost. We will always have tomorrow, but meanwhile, today's time inventory has evaporated.

This isn't such a problem when you work for a company. You get paid as long as you show up. If the boss can't hand over an assignment because the papers are buried somewhere under his coffee mug or he says he is too inundated in phone messages and emails to answer you, it waits till tomorrow or even later. This may increase stress and pressure down the road, but for today, you simply work on something else or clean out files. Or stop by Starbucks for twenty minutes. When a freelance client behaves in the same way, your inventory is wilting, evaporating into the garbage dumpster of the universe.

One way to fill unassigned time is with marketing projects. You've got to keep marketing. But it's so easy to give such preference to marketing that you lose sight of the billable time as it evaporates.

Let's not forget one truth for the solopro: *It's all about doing paying work.*

How do I make sure I get paid promptly?

You get paid promptly by invoicing promptly. If you don't care enough to invoice at each step along the way as soon as permitted under your agreement, don't expect them to come looking for you, waving your check. It doesn't look greedy or presumptuous to present your invoice. It simply looks businesslike. I email most invoices, but I have no problem presenting them in person if the occasion permits.

How do I prepare an invoice?

The creation of electronic letterhead could be done at any time, even on day one. Simply take the text of your business card, put it at the top of a Word file and save as letterhead.

To create an invoice, open the Letterhead file. Then add the following, substituting your facts as necessary:

Date

Name, company, address of client

"Invoice," centered

RE: Brief description of project

Any relevant milestones or measures with cost

Terms of payment (optional but wise)
Example:

10 hours @ $50 per hour ………………….…. ………….$500.00

or
Phase 1 …………………….…......…..……………..$2,500.00

Phase 2……………………………………………….$500.00

Total …………………..…………………..………..$3,000.00

Payment due upon receipt of this invoice.
Thank you.

Social Security number or Business ID number (optional, but it often saves time)

That's it! It's ready to email as an attached document, preferably saved and sent as a PDF to avoid risk of any alterations, such as formatting glitches, on the client end. (Sometimes I bill by PayPal rather than the typical invoice if the client agrees to it).

Then keep complete records of everything you do.

Collections 101: Get what you've earned

You may wish to combine a phone call with your invoice if you think there is any chance it may not have gone through (your email is under the weather). Whether you get them on the phone or leave a voicemail message, just confirm as you do when emailing actual work: "Hi, Jim, Just calling to let you know I've sent you the invoice. Please let me know if it doesn't show up or if there are any questions. Thanks." Then conclude with your phone number.

Any agreements should state that payment is due upon receipt or other language that stresses promptness. You can refer to this language in any required follow-up.

Note the due date on your print or electronic calendar, such as Outlook, for follow-up if payment has not been received.

Check off all payments from your list of payments due or in your online accounting program as soon as they arrive and cash checks immediately. This is especially valid for small businesses where your client also maintains the books. Collecting promptly must not be important to you if you don't cash the check, right? Demonstrate to your client that you mean business.

Swing into action promptly after payment is due but it hasn't been received. You can start by forwarding to the same client your original email requesting payment. If you send it as a forward, your original invoice document will be attached.

Next step is to wait a day or two and then phone to ask in a friendly tone if payment has been mailed. The U.S. Postal Service once or twice literally required more than two weeks to transport a check from Chicago to my Chicago suburb. Don't assume the worst—the check may actually be in the mail.

If the client lost the invoice, doesn't remember, or whatever, immediately forward to them the email you previously sent with the invoice attachment. This politely and without confrontation proves that you already sent them the invoice.

The more unresponsive they become, the tougher you must become. I've only had one client in arrears on a significant sum. I started calling daily and they came through with my check, probably to shut me up.

There are other paths—hiring an attorney and small-claims court come to mind. However, these cost money and may not be effective. (In fact, they probably *won't* be effective, in part because you may have a global clientele.) Start with the way that is free—your own phone calls.

A real-life story

I once had a bad feeling about a client for whom I had completed a project. I phoned them every single day until they put the check in the mail. They had more important creditors I'm sure but I was the biggest annoyance. In this case the squeaky wheel got the grease.

You may think that small claims court is the answer. I don't know about that. I've never been to small claims court. I simply knew that what I was owed (about $2,500) would not be a big deal to the courts or to an attorney—legal fees could eat up the full amount. While I could perhaps learn to represent myself in small claims, the aggravation would consume too much of my energy and attention. So I aggravated them instead.

It worked!

What if I make them so angry they never give me another assignment? That's all for the best. You don't want to work for people who don't pay. Never work for them again unless you are paid in full up-front. Next!

What if they say bad things about me to others? There's nothing *bad* about collecting the money you are owed. For them to tell people that you are too persistent in collecting requires them to tell people they avoid paying their bills. Why would they do that?

How to improve collection practices

When you are a solopro freelancer or consultant, there are worse things than having no work to do.

Number one on the list is working hard but not getting paid.

So here are some tips to solve the problem.

Structure payment to get as much as possible up front or at least along the way. After you solve the client's problem and deliver the goods, you are just another creditor on their list.

Policy. One effective strategy is to require full payment (or at least one-half) up front. When asked why, practitioners of this approach say, "It is our policy."

No debate, it's just policy.

Obviously, for a single-person business, policy doesn't require any vote or top-executive decision back at the office. An individual can change *policy* at will.

But calling it *policy* cuts off uncomfortable discussion.

Those who follow this path tend to be highly confident, ready to cut their losses and proceed to the next prospect.

They remind themselves it is better to have no work and to spend time prospecting (for instance, telephoning) than it is to use up time, your most limited and precious resource, to do work that doesn't pay on time and may never pay.

Sometimes the largest companies are the worst. A prospect may say it's not their policy (they too have *policies!*) to pay immediately. You see this most frequently at large companies with lots of rules and lots of prestige.

Before the recession, big-company executives, when challenged by solopros awaiting payment, would laugh and say, "Well of course we're good for the money." Then freelancers would end up waiting sixty to ninety days to get paid. I've heard stories of big companies refusing to pay after the work is done and forcing the individual to settle for fifty cents on the dollar. Simply because they can.

Some solopros add a penalty percentage for late payments. Bad idea unless you want to function as a financing company. If clients are agreeable towards paying a penalty, they recast you as a source of capital for which they are paying interest. You loan them your fees and they pay when they're good and ready. Seems totally legit to them since they are agreeing to pay the additional fees. No rush for them to pay if they don't mind compound interest.

Postponing payment is now a financial decision, not theft. (Normally it is stealing when you take a service and don't pay for it.) Yay! You're a financing company!

How can I assure that my income is stable as a solopro?

Sorry, you can't. You may earn less than at a corporate job, you may earn much more. But you will never have the income stability you had at a corporate job.

If you want stability, get a regular job. Or take a permanent part-time job to assure some steady income, though lately, no job is truly stable.

Yes, for a while you may seem to have a stable income from solopro work. Some freelancers/consultants obtain long-term assignments and appear to have the same stability of income as they had in their regular job.

But here's the difference: That *permanent assignment* can disappear at any time and for any reason. The client may terminate the project, the department that hired you, the product, the function, or anything else. They may want fresh blood. The person who selected you may have left for another job and the replacement may bring in his own person or otherwise declare *a new era of excellence*, as symbolized by new solopros.

Someone may call to tell you this. Or they may never get back to you until you leave persistent voicemail messages about starting the next cycle of your recurring assignment.

In a regular job, you would have probably heard the rumors, read memos upside down on the supervisor's desk, or seen mysterious people meet with the boss behind closed doors. When you're off premises, there's no way to know what is going to happen until it happens.

How do I assure that I will have grocery money by this weekend?

Consulting/freelancing may do the job of raising immediate cash—if you are fortunate enough to get an assignment and you can convince them to pay the first installment with an overnight check or with electronic payment such as PayPal.

However, many companies are not set up to pay that quickly. Your desperation diminishes you in their eyes and makes them value you and your work less.

So the answer is to be highly selective in looking for assignments that do not have a lag time between the work and payment (unlike both corporate employment and much freelance/corporate work—even once the assignments have been obtained.) The only way to know you will have money by the weekend is to clarify this boldly before taking on the work. Not many projects promise both an immediate go-ahead and immediate payment. Proceed with caution. I'm not optimistic that you'll find what you need.

Instead, consider babysitting, childcare, yard work, and similar chores.

In the long-run, solopros must market consistently and set aside funds to meet future expenses. Even when you get a large, exciting check, think twice about spending it all. This applies even to paying down your charge card. Sounds like the responsible thing to do, but if your income is erratic, you may not have enough money to pay even the minimum next month.

To the point:

- There are three common ways to bill for solopro services: by the hour, a flat rate by the project, and by the value of the work delivered. Each of the three has both pluses and minuses.

- The inventory of a solopro consists of time. Value and conserve your time as the precious resource it is.

- Schedule project deliverables and payment milestones to collect as much of the fee as possible as early as possible. If you deliver everything before any payment is received, they are less motivated to pay. Other invoices they have received may take precedence over yours.

- Invoice and follow up on payments promptly to assure

prompt payment. This is intrinsic to being a grown-up professional.

- Your objective is payment, not maintaining the goodwill of deadbeats. You are in business to make money. Nothing wrong with that. Nothing to apologize for.

Step 6

Manage Yourself: Do the Work and Manage Your Time

We've already seen how being a solopro freelancer or consultant requires lots of marketing, not just at the beginning but for as long as it is your career.

In addition, it requires strong management skills . . . and the person you most need to manage is yourself. If you've been working in a corporate cubicle, whether literally or figuratively, you may be light in terms of self-management. You've learned to lean back into deadlines set by others and may find moving ahead on your own business horrendously challenging.

The problem may resolve itself, at least partially, as you land clients and set deadlines with their cooperation. I've known freelancers who proclaim to a client that they will have the completed assignment out by tomorrow at 9 A.M. And then they actually do it. The client, I am told, is amazed. And quite possible, I am not told, amused. If the situation is not a crisis, there's something off kilter about this. Here's what's off kilter: The solopro has problems managing himself and needs to promise unnecessarily tight deadlines to focus himself.

Some solopros do the exact opposite: They take a task that requires limited time but set the deadline weeks into the future so the client thinks they are very busy and very important even though their time is not fully booked. Some do the work immediately but let it age on their desk before submitting it. Others wait weeks until the night before the deadline so they can enjoy the adrenaline rush.

It takes all kinds of people to make the world go round. Some of these people function more effectively than others.

However, it all illustrates some of the problems in the realm of self-management. This chapter discusses additional problems, and throughout your career you'll run across even more of them in your own life.

What to do on Day One?

I am.

These are the most powerful words a new freelancer or consultant can say (of course, when supplemented with a word or phrase that completes the thought). For instance, "I am a training consultant." Or, "I am a writer." Or, to tweak the pattern slightly, "I design," or "I advise," or "I plan."

What all these statements have in common is that they state who you are in the present tense.

Take a stand—now.

Now I'm not speaking as my former-English-teacher self here. It's not the grammar, it's the sense of identity that comes from telling yourself, and telling others, who you are.

Consider the alternative, a vague statement of what you may do in the future. "I'm thinking of …" or "I'd kind of like to …" or "I'm looking into…" or "Maybe I'll…"

The difference seems slight at first. But in terms of moving a business forward, the difference is huge. It takes a certain decisiveness to tell the world what you do in the present tense.

Say it aloud. When networking or simply talking to friends, family, and acquaintances, use the present tense. At the beginning—and perhaps even after you've been at the business for a while—it can be difficult. You may have to take this step consciously, thinking about what you say to make the change.

When you speak vaguely about the future, no one can challenge or even question you. People respond with an equally vague—but positive—response: "That's nice." Or, "Sounds good." Or, "Great idea."

Wimps describe their business in future tense. But future statements don't engage others on either a practical or a spiritual plane. If you are looking for serendipity (unexpected opportunity!), this won't coax its appearance.

What you say is not etched in stone. There is nothing weak or embarrassing about refining your mission over time. Even after you print business cards or create websites, your visions continue to evolve. But speaking in the present tense helps you try on an identity and gauge how it fits.

At this point you may be thinking about elevator speeches and two-minute intros. While crafting snappy marketing messages may be in your future, for now, simply stating what you do in a word or two, in the present tense, is a brave step.

What is full-time work for a freelancer or consultant?

One downside of self-employment is that there's no one to set your hours except you. And when you work for yourself, you may have the most unforgiving taskmaster of all.

I find myself sorely tempted to translate my efforts into number of hours worked to determine if I am working *enough*.

When I worked in an office for a boss, I measured hours from the time I got to my desk to the time I turned off my desk lamp and left. If I gabbed with someone or surfed the web for inspiration, I didn't subtract it. So it was easy to *work* an eight-hour day and I frequently *worked* ten hours. I could feel good about a fifty-hour work week no matter how little I accomplished. In fact, I had days where I was ill but I went to my desk to avoid using sick leave, accomplishing nothing all day.

When I switched over to self-employment, I found it impossible to separate work from personal so I became continually more rigid in defining what work is. My schedule always fell short of my goals no matter how hard I tried!

Then I learned an enormously comforting truth from various experts and Internet pals. A full workweek for a freelancer or consultant consists of only twenty to twenty-five billable hours, not forty. This allows unpaid time for email, marketing, invoicing, administration, etc. within the workweek. As a result, a week consisting of twenty-five billable hours represents a substantial amount of work (like it is!) rather than a laid-back week. And while a week of forty billable hours is physically possible, it probably takes place at the expense of office tasks and marketing that must be reassigned to others or delayed.

As you start a new freelance/consulting practice, you may have no billable hours but may devote all your work hours to marketing. This can make the separation of work and personal time more hazy. As the days pass by and you maintain your marketing focus with modest initial results, the boundary between work and play becomes less distinct.

How people handle this distinction varies. One way is to distinguish more clearly between your work schedule (perhaps nine to five) and leisure hours and to assign activities rigidly to the appropriate time slots. The advantage here is that you can turn off work at 5 P.M. and proceed to the other parts of your life.

Then there is the opposite path. Blending *work* with *personal* in a rather seamless way can be the ultimate in living life if you've chosen to break away from payroll situations where others call all the shots.

All in all, it comes back to being reasonable with yourself. We think of the Golden Rule (*Do unto others as you would have them do unto you*) as meaning to be as kind to others as you would have them be towards you. But practice it in reverse as well: *Do unto yourself with as much love as you give unto others.*

What's the best way to manage daily quotas?

Do you thrive on writing long to-do lists and crossing off items one by one? If you regularly set daily goals, eventually (after like maybe the first or second day) you'll have a day when you fail to reach all your goals. No matter how conscientiously you strive to dial your target number of calls each day, eventually you'll have a day where you fall short.

Then you face the big question: Are you going to add today's shortfall to tomorrow's quota or are you going to start fresh tomorrow?

Start fresh tomorrow! After all, there's a reason you missed your goal today. Maybe other tasks were higher priority. Or you didn't feel well. Or you simply weren't in the mood. Quite possibly your goal was too big for a single day.

It is plenty just to overcome these obstacles sufficiently to handle tomorrow's list without piling on more work left over from today. And if these tasks keep adding up, you'll get to the point where you dread getting out of bed the next morning.

During my life, I've committed to all sorts of New Year's, birthday, school year, and other daily resolutions, such as vocabulary development and acne treatment routines in my teens. Sit-ups in my twenties. Packing lunches the night before in my thirties and forties. Currently it's sorting through my mail and paper pile. Or reciting affirmations.

Start where you are. You are not behind. I live (somewhat) by this philosophy, stated by Marla Cilley, the Flylady (flylady.net). She has a great system for getting stuff done around the house and in life in general. Every day she assigns a homemaking task or two, and if you don't finish today's, you simply go on to tomorrow's tomorrow. No saving up tasks so you can kill yourself with effort someday down the road.

Other experts have different rules to measure different types of life achievements. Julia Cameron in *The Artist's Way* recommends three pages of free writing each morning to stimulate creativity and conquer writer's block—even if your art form of choice does not include writing. Others prefer to write a certain number of pages each month. In effect, the latter choice gives us permission to procrastinate for weeks and then start writing like crazy on the twenty-seventh. Julia's way requires more writing but is easier to accomplish, especially if you allow any daily shortfalls to vanish from memory.

So what doesn't get done today, such as your self-imposed daily assignment of marketing phone calls, just let it stay undone (as much as is reasonably possible). Start fresh tomorrow. As Scarlett O'Hara said, "Tomorrow is another day."

Let tomorrow truly be a new day, not today's make-up day.

What is the second task each day for a solopro?

As discussed in Step 5, the first task of the day is to send out any invoices that are due. Now on to the second task. Every evening as you leave your desk or workshop, determine your top priority for the next day. Place it on your desk, ready to begin, and get started first thing in the morning. This might be a must-do but potentially messy phone call or continuing on with a major project. Starting the day with your most important work eases the rest of your day and makes you feel virtuous besides.

The second task may be marketing. At times—such as in the beginning—you'll spend far more time on marketing than on completing assignments. At other times, your top priority is the client work you have already agreed to perform. You must schedule enough time to do it well, and you must schedule it promptly to complete projects by deadline. You may tell yourself (as I have done many a time), that you work best under pressure. Then you can procrastinate to your heart's delight.

But if you get a fast start, you can do a much better job. You can get better input from others when you give them a little lead time to respond. You can explore ideas that will require research or creative sleeping on it. You'll enjoy the intellectual stimulation of your chosen profession and feel a lot less stress.

Retrain yourself to work well without the external whip of last-minute pressures. Your work product will improve and so will your pleasure.

By the way, if you are dividing your time between marketing (especially phoning) and paying assignments, it may be easiest to market during the day when prospects are in their offices and to do paying projects in the evening when there are fewer distractions from others.

I'm employed full-time. How can I start to solopro on the side?

Let's start with a short quiz and your possible answers:

1. Is your intended practice a conflict of interest with your job? Is it important *for any reason* that your boss not find out what you are doing?

If so, I recommend not doing it. If you want to make some extra money, find an undertaking that simply generates cash but in no way relates to your work. Even if you want to pursue your practice so you can eventually quit your job, identify activities for the time being, whether paying or preparatory, that are not in conflict. This may be volunteer work, college or other coursework, assembling a portfolio, or work in another industry. You may take on leadership roles in industry organizations (ideally, with your company paying your dues and providing in-house support), or develop your website and other marketing efforts, or write a book to establish your expertise (perhaps for publication after you resign your day job).

You may be tempted to ask potential clients to keep your secret. Don't. This behavior broadcasts that you lack integrity. A real turnoff.

2. Do you have time now to do the work?

Be realistic. If you have loads of energy and can work around the clock, it may be okay to take on lots of work and agree to tight deadlines. But don't commit to what you can't do. Rather than build your reputation, this will harm it. You'll feel bad about your service and add enormous stress to your life.

3. When can you contact clients?

Starting to freelance/consult while still employed works best if you can take phone calls during the day. Be honest here. Can you answer your cell phone and talk openly? Incomplete answers that don't tip off the coworker in the next cubicle don't cut it. You must be able to concentrate fully on callbacks and discuss issues in depth.

If your only problem is how to phone prospects during office hours, target clients in other time zones. For instance, if you live in the U.S. Eastern Time zone, try to work early flextime and leave the office at 3 P.M. This is noon in California. That's five business hours every day that you are available.

Conversely, if you live in the Pacific Time zone, get on the phone at 5:30 A.M. and have a few hours of contact time with the East Coast before you go to the office.

If the service you offer appeals to companies around the world, your opportunities are even greater. Whatever time it is in your area, it's daylight somewhere else. See too if you can switch your day job to night or weekend hours so you are available during the workday for your new endeavor.

4. What will you tell prospects and clients if you are not available when they want to talk?

Since you are honest (you are, aren't you?), tell the truth. "I am serious about my solopro work and dedicated to meeting your deadlines with the highest quality work. However, at this time I am also working a day job."

Or depending on your job and its role in your life, you may choose to say, "I am working onsite tomorrow but I can schedule a call to you between noon and 1 P.M. I can also review my voice mail during this time period and follow up with you."

In practice, the more they communicate with you via email, the easier it is to work client service into your schedule. You may want to answer them during breaks or lunch during the work day, or you may write to them during the odd hours they are not at their desks.

How can I deal with discouragement?

The best way to avoid discouragement is to keep your expectations realistic. Freelancing/consulting is not likely to make you instantly rich, to fill your days with top-paying assignments from the outset, or to return a check in tomorrow's mail. It can take an extended period to really kick in and offer enough of the well-paying, interesting clients you want.

That's how life is.

I find that my level of discouragement absolutely correlates with how tired I am. If I am discouraged, I go to bed early. It makes all the difference in the world. The cure may be different for you: eat healthier, take vitamins, walk along the seashore, exercise, listen to music.

Stay close to friends. If you're like me, you need people who will hear out your complaints and even endure your self-pity. Without an office, you may have to search out these people.

Understand why you are discouraged. Years ago I tried counseling and antidepressants, in large part because of marketing frustrations as a solopro. Every other week I'd meet with my social worker to recite how many prospecting calls I had made, what people had said, how many mailings I had sent out, and how many sales meetings I had scheduled. As you may suspect, the social worker knew less about what I was doing than I did, though I was looking for her to validate if I had done *enough*. In my case, I should have gone with a marketing coach instead of a social worker. (But this depends on the individual—counseling or even medications may be right for you. Consult professionals.)

To the point:

- Since you won't have an employee manual or a boss, you'll need self-discipline to accomplish all you need to get done.

- A typical solopro workweek consists of only twenty to twenty-five billable hours. Unpaid administrative, marketing, networking, and self-development tasks will claim the remaining hours.

- Start your to-do list fresh every day. Don't carry over today's unachieved daily goals for phone calling or other marketing activities to add to tomorrow's goals because you will soon be overwhelmed.

• Are you thinking of starting your freelance/consulting practice on the side as a supplement to your full-time job? Avoid conflicts of interest with your day work so balancing the two will be more comfortable and less secretive. Also consider how the time demands and client interaction will fit into your life.

Step 7

Start Fast! Get Up and Running in One Day

You made the right decision when you started reading this book and kept on reading. You've seen that it's okay to start imperfectly. Now simply follow along—you can get your business up and running in a single day.

Shut the door, quit scanning incoming email, and let's get your solopro practice under way today.

Let me make many of your decisions.

High-priced advisors want to make it seem like every decision is critical. You can do tens of thousands of dollars' worth of research and listen to focus groups and measure interviewees' heart rates and sweat to determine the best color for your logo. But that's overkill for an individual practice that is just starting out. Whatever you choose, it doesn't much matter and it can be changed at any time.

For your logo, I say *blue*. Why? Because most people like blue and just as important, because I say so. The alternative is to pass hours playing on your computer to discover just the right shade. Believe me, it makes no difference.

Of course, go ahead and implement any relevant decisions you have already made. You know your business better than anyone else, even if you don't know everything about it at this time.

The steps listed here may take less than eight hours or they may take more. Actual time required depends on how many decisions you have already made and your writing and computer skills. My objective is for you to put all the steps in place quickly so you can go on to active marketing. If the process extends to nine hours, heaven forbid, that's okay. You can go back to thinking for yourself as soon as you're done.

Implement concrete steps, ditch the soul searching.

These fifteen steps are purely about getting things done. Today is for action, not theoretical considerations or soul searching.

Suspend your perfectionism.

You can tweak, improve, re-do all of these tasks tomorrow, and every tomorrow thereafter if you wish. Just get them done today.

Take other work off the table, literally or figuratively.

Today's about following the list. Don't get distracted by other projects.

Adjust this list as necessary for your unique situation.

For instance, I suggest postponing your website. However, if you plan to develop corporate websites professionally, your own website will have to be moved towards the top of the list and must be done especially well.

But that does not mean it has to be done today. Start marketing before you have the perfect website. It's quite common to devote ourselves to what we do well (in your case, websites) so we can postpone what we fear. Marketing? Phoning? Paying assignments for strangers?

The checklist

Here are the fifteen steps to get your solopro freelance/consulting practice up and running on Day One.

Before you get started, note that:

• The time ranges are only suggestions. Your experience may differ. That's OK.

• Allow yourself to work fast. None of your decisions is set in concrete. You can tweak anything and everything tomorrow and for as many additional tomorrows as you wish.

• The "next steps" provide some guidance on how to revisit and flesh out your initial decisions. They are meant to be postponed. You may want to store these ideas in the nooks and crannies of your brain for consideration as you drive, jog, fold laundry, or simply procrastinate in the future.

1. Determine the service you offer. [5–15 minutes]
2. Determine your job title. [5–15 minutes]
3. Create or update your LinkedIn profile [30–45 minutes]
4. Create a signature for your email. [10–20 minutes]
5. Develop your logo. [30–45 minutes]
6. Create your business card. [30–45 minutes]
7. Record a new message for your voicemail or answering machine. [5–15 minutes]
8. Format your database. [10–20 minutes]
9. Prepare an initial telephone script for speaking to prospects. [20–40 minutes]
10. Prepare a phone script for when you reach

voicemail. [10–20 minutes]
11. Prepare email templates for following up on your
    calls. [30–50 minutes]
12. Make a list of the first prospects you will contact.
    [60–90 minutes]
13. Determine your initial pay rate. [10–25 minutes]
14. Inform your family, friends, colleagues, email lists
    and already-established online social networks
    about your new business. [30–40 minutes]
15. Join an online forum that offers quick feedback
    from your peers. [20–30 minutes]

1. Determine the service you offer.

You probably have a sense already of what service you offer.

Now state it in a few words, perhaps as few as one. If you
know your niche, include it in your service statement. If not,
start simple, choosing a broader concept such as graphics design, writing, marketing, coaching, or project management.

If you don't even have a concept in mind, look at your last
job. Your practice may be exactly what you did in your last
payroll job or it can be an element of this job.

If you are deeply at sea here, you may wish to sit at the
kitchen table and list out concepts by the hour. Or go out
and talk to others, read, refresh yourself on a nature trail, etc.
Postponing this decision is fine. It may be just right for you.
However, it will postpone making contact with others and
actually pinning down assignments.

You need not stay with this service title forever. Some of
the best and brightest continue to refine—or even recreate—
their direction multiple times over their careers.

I suggest you choose a simple word at least for now and
let your questions and concerns swirl around at some level in
your mind for further consideration.

When the time is right, you can adjust or totally change this decision.

Next steps

- Test the idea on yourself. How do you feel when you tell people what you do? Does it feel right?

- Allow yourself to test both the general concept of your service and the specific words you use to describe it as you offer your services in the marketplace.

- As you contact prospects, be sensitive to their reactions. Can you sense how your market responds to your service title?

- Ask friends, friendly clients, and professional online groups in which you participate for their feedback.

- Feel free to reconsider what service you offer as you refine your business concept. No decision is irrevocable!

2. Determine your job title.

Your job title may be exactly the same as the service you offer (see step 1 above), but more than likely, you'll tweak it. For instance, *design* will become *designer* and *writing* morphs to...*writer.*

The same complicated issues that present themselves in step 1 can continue into this step. I urge you to keep this simple and work from your previous decision.

I know a writer who has been freelancing for decades. He labels himself simply as *Writer* on his business card. I was surprised when I first saw his card, but he's doing quite well, thank you.

Go for clarity. Nothing cute like *Chief Imagineer* or *Head Buffoon.*

Next steps

- As with your service, feel free to reconsider your title as you develop and refine your business.

- Update your business card, LinkedIn profile, voicemail message, elevator speech, social media profiles, etc. every time you change your title.

3. Create or update your LinkedIn profile.

Many people assume that the starting place for building a business is the website. Not a bad idea if you know how to set it up and can get it done quickly.

However, it's more important to have a presence on LinkedIn. This can be instead of or in addition to a website.

LinkedIn is necessary because virtually anyone who hires freelancers and consultants for business assignments knows how to use LinkedIn. My favorite aspect of LinkedIn is the way it provides the same data as a formal résumé, especially work history and education. Solopros may appear all over the Internet and be prominent in Google searches, but LinkedIn is the only place where people researching you can figure out the facts.

The basics of LinkedIn are highly intuitive and you can get your profile up in as little as thirty minutes, especially if you've already written a résumé.

Next steps

- Over time, continue to improve your LinkedIn profile. Join LinkedIn groups. Fill in more fields and flesh out what you have already posted. Keep your profile and your status field up-to-date. In particular, invite clients and other professional contacts to "connect" with you.

- Make your own decisions as to what's important and where to invest your time. LinkedIn pressures users to achieve scores of 100% by using all their features, including the solicitation of recommendations praising your work. If you have someone you know will post a recommendation, shoot them an email requesting help. If no names come to mind—or your contacts need prompting on what to write or even pre-written copy that you provide to them—postpone this element for a later time. (By the way, it's totally ethical to write the recommendation as long as they endorse it by submitting it independently. A well-done recommendation relates specifics about the service you provide and your work habits, not just that you're a nice guy.)

- If you want a website, start with a single page that largely reworks your LinkedIn content. You eventually will want to post a more sophisticated website. Polished websites often take months or even years to complete, not necessarily because the technical side is so difficult (you may want to hire a pro if the tech part intimidates you), but because committing our identity in this way is such a confounding psychological hurdle.

4. Create a signature for your email.

This is the block of information about you that will appear automatically at the end of all your emails, publicizing your service with every message you send.

Type out:

Your name | Title or service you offer

Email address | Telephone number

City and state

Link to LinkedIn profile or website

Obviously, you must select a phone number for business use right now. For many people, it is their cell phone number. This is the best choice when you have your own private phone and when you expect to take calls while out of the office. You may prefer to use your home phone number if that has been your practice in the past or if that plan is more economical, but you'll want to be sure that anyone answering the line handles messages professionally and that the rest of the family doesn't mind a business message when incoming calls go to voicemail. If you plan to acquire another phone line for business purposes, do this as soon as possible so all the contacts you make receive the right number from the start.

You may wish to add your street address if this is useful to others, but there's the (remote!) possibility that a client may turn up at your house unexpected. Showing the city and state is sufficient for most purposes. And it indicates to contacts your time zone so they can determine when to phone you.

Add your fax number if you wish, but it's most likely unnecessary digital clutter.

Next steps

- Update this signature as needed.

- Add an extra line, if you wish, devoted to current information, such as a recent award, milestone, or published article.

5. Develop your logo.

It will consist of your name.

Use Verdana (a font developed for electronic communications) and make it blue. Make it bold.

It will look like this (but blue!):

Your Name

Next steps

- Update as needed.

- Obviously, there's room for lots of creativity here. Caution: logos can claim a huge expenditure in terms of time and money. It's perfectly OK to wait until your sense of what your business is all about matures before you get too deep into this.

- When you are ready for a logo, consider hiring a pro.

- On the other hand, you may find you have no use for your logo, especially if you order your business cards from an online service that offers fill-in-the-blank templates. If that's the case, invest no further time or money in logo development.

6. Create your business card.

Copy your signature (step 4) and your logo (step 5), combining lines as necessary and centering in the space available. Use the features of your word processing software to customize the layout to the brand of card stock you have on hand.

Run a sample page on plain paper to make sure the printing lines up correctly with the perforated card stock and then print a single page. If you don't have special card stock on hand, simply save the file, all prepared to print later. Purchase plain white card stock and print off cards a page at a time as needed.

If you don't want to print them yourself, use a service such as www.vistaprint.com. Select a free, simple design that is predominantly blue. Fill in the blanks, proofread, order. The cards will show up at your front door in only a few days.

Remember that even though this is labeled as "free" (if you

allow their logo on the back of the cards), you will pay for shipping and handling. Still, the expense is minor and in my experience, delivery has been fast.

Leave the back of the cards blank for handwritten notes. I prefer to pay a few bucks extra so there is no advertising on the back. Real classy!

Next steps

- Prepare a page or two of new cards as needed.

- If it's right for your business and your desired clients, upgrade to professionally designed and printed cards once the money's coming in. Order only the amount you think you can use in one year, unless the price breaks by quantity make a large order cost effective. 250 cards should be more than enough unless you attend many conferences and other live networking events.

7. Record a new message for your voicemail or answering machine.

This is a subtle way to let friends, relatives, and contacts of all sorts know what you do, while assuring prospects that they got the right number.

Again, don't go cute or funny. You want clarity.

Here's a possible script that can be expanded and fine-tuned as you clarify your service offerings and niche:

> *Hello, you've reached [name], [job title]. Please leave a complete message and I'll call you back as soon as possible.*

> You can also add a sentence after your job title, such as, *I look forward to discussing how I can help you … [fill in the blank].*

You may meet resistance on such a message if you share this phone line with your family, but ask them what they're comfortable with.

Next steps

- Add this message to all phone lines you will use for business purposes, including cell phones.

- Update message as needed.

- Consider adding a brief, informational sales message to your voicemail such as, "I have now added crisis management to my publicity offerings."

- Customize your message with relevant temporary or seasonal information, such as "Avoid the April rush. Start your tax planning early." However, only use a time-sensitive message if you will change it again when it becomes out of date!

8. Format your database.

When you start contacting possible clients, you'll want to record all relevant data in a single place. Don't waste time on evaluating, purchasing, installing, and mastering database software. Start where you are.

If you already have contact management software, use it. If you own and know Microsoft Access, use it. Microsoft Excel or equivalents are also acceptable at the beginning. (I've never personally had the need to upgrade beyond this level. A recurring emailed newsletter or other mass marketing effort is implemented on Aweber, Constant Contact, MailChimp, or a similar service, not from your own computer.)

If at all possible, create this database on your computer, not on paper. This makes it easily searchable and much simpler to work with.

Determine the fields you will need to record. Here's an initial list for your consideration:

Prefixes: Mr./Ms./Dr.

First name

Last name

Suffixes: Jr./Sr./III

Name of company

Job title

Street address, line 1

Street address, line 2

City

State

Zip

Country

Phone

Fax

Email address

Corporate website

Date of first contact

Source of contact information

Comments/notes

Niche/specialty (theirs)

Next contact activity

Next contact date

As you make lots of contacts, filling in each field is time-consuming. Don't make the task any more cumbersome than it needs to be. Fill in only the fields you think you will use. Some of the data won't be available for everyone so leave fields blank to be completed later as needed.

If you plan special marketing campaigns, such as individualized print letters or a series of print postcards, you may wish to collect and format data so it is ready to go when you are ready to implement. If you aren't sure or have no definite plans, don't worry about it. Allow data collection to be as simple as possible. Once you start phoning, you'll be glad you did.

When I started, I recorded every fax number I found. However, this was years ago, and even then, I rarely faxed. Now I only record the fax number when I think I'll need it. Which is never.

You must be accurate in every piece of data you record. There's no point in keying in incorrect phone numbers or email addresses. Close doesn't count, this ain't horseshoes.

Next steps

- Maintain the database consistently. Ideally, add data after each call. At a minimum, make rough written notes after each call and key them all in the same day.

- Someday in the future, you may decide to switch over to sophisticated, sales-oriented software.

9. Prepare an initial telephone script for speaking to prospects.

I use the word *script* with great trepidation because the last thing you want is to sound scripted. After all, you're talking about yourself, a topic on which you have in-depth, first-hand knowledge. So don't sound like a stilted telemarketer who would be thrown off her canned presentation by an enthusiastic *yes!* midway through.

It's better to stumble when talking than to sound scripted. Much more genuine. If you are having trouble remembering what to say, put the script in the trash can. Don't just keep nervously repeating the exact script robot-style. If you have a slight lapse, simply keep going conversationally.

Consider . . . you've had years of experience talking on the phone and you don't recall any of your slips of tongue over the years or the *ahs* and *uhms* or even asking, "What was I saying?" Just keep going. Try slouching in your chair to achieve a relaxed conversational tone or smiling without an audience to convey enthusiasm.

Your mission is to learn about their needs and inform them of your services. To make their lives better by being useful, which starts with being honest. It's not to utter some killer phrase that magically enslaves them to your captivating offer.

Consider the following template:

> *Hi, this is [name]. I [what you do]. Do you ever use such services?*

If they say *yes*, ask a follow-up question to clarify what types of projects they have and if they have any needs on the horizon. As you complete the conversation, offer to send an email with further information.

If they say *no*, they have no need for freelance or consulting at this time or they never use these services, suggest you'll send a follow-up email in case their needs change.

This line of conversation is nothing fancy, but it gets the job done.

Next steps

- As you make calls and become more comfortable with the process, what you say will evolve.

- Keep a mental or written list of the phrases and approaches that seem most effective.

- Keep a mental or written list of ways to keep your calls fresh, conversational, service-oriented, and effective.

10. Prepare a phone script for when you reach voicemail.

Many of your calls will roll over to voicemail. This is a terrific opportunity to leave a message about what you do, informing a potential prospect of your services.

Some "experts" recommend hanging up and trying again later. No! I recommend leaving a message for several reasons:

- Nothing positive can possibly happen if you leave no message.

- People who are interested will *want to* return your call.

- People record your information and either use it themselves at a later date or pass it on to colleagues. Believe it or not, I've received valuable phone calls from people to whom I was referred by someone I've never talked to. (Ask people where they got your name if you don't already know.)

- You have the chance to give your spiel without interruption.

- It's great practice for delivering your message.

In short, if you have something important to say—and you do, or else you wouldn't be calling!—go ahead and leave a message.

This script will be similar to the one in step 9, but make sure to ask them to call back. State your name and phone number clearly, both at the beginning and the end of the call. If you have their email address, tell them you will follow up with an email explanation of your services. Then send the email immediately.

Next steps

- As you become more comfortable making calls, you will develop a feel for what works for you. Adapt your script accordingly.

11. Prepare email templates for following up on your calls.

The initial paragraph will have a casual tone, such as the following:

> *Hi, Tom. I'm so glad we were able to discuss how my [fill in the blank] services may be of use to you. Here is the email we discussed. Please let me know if I can provide any further information.*

OR

> *Hi, Tom. I'm so sorry my call missed you today. I phoned to discuss how my [fill in the blank] services may be of use to you. Here is the email I promised in my message. Please let me know if I can provide any further information.*

This is followed by:

> *Heading centered, in bold*
>
> *Your name, service*
>
> *Subservice 1 ~ Subservice 2 ~ Subservice 3*
>
> *[1-3 sentences about the services you offer]*

My qualifications include:

[3 bullets from your résumé]

Additional information appears on my LinkedIn profile: [insert link to profile]

Let's discuss your [service] needs. Simply phone me at 123-456-7899 so we can proceed.

I hope we can work together soon.

Thank you,

[your first name]

Your email signature

Send all follow-up immediately. It won't take long to customize your email template so send it right out. If you agree to email (or mail) work samples or other information, take care of that too.

Review the email each time you send it, adapting it as appropriate. You may add a note about your connection to the prospect, such as mutual membership in a professional organization or the contact who gave you the referral.

Record all contact information, including any promised follow-up scheduled for the future, in your contact database. Also note promised follow-up in your daily planner, calendar, task management program, or Outlook schedule to assure you follow through.

Next steps

- Keep expanding and improving this email. (See Appendix 1 for one of my typical emails that I have developed over time.)

- Develop variations for multiple niches as needed. Save

each version with a descriptive file name so you can find it easily.

12. Make a list of the first prospects you will contact.

Tomorrow you'll start telephoning, so most important to getting your marketing under way is an initial calling list. Start with your Rolodex, either your literal file of phone numbers or the Rolodex in your brain. If your specialty in some ways echoes past work experience, you should already have some potential contacts in mind.

If you belong to professional organizations, grab your print membership directories or go to their websites to cull some names.

Don't start with the biggest company or most important individual in the field. Warm up with contacts that may pan out but don't matter in the long run. Save more crucial contacts for later in the game when you are more comfortable on the phone.

Next steps

- Find more names! Always be on the lookout for people to contact.

- Look back through this report for lots of ideas on how to find people to contact.

- As you read the local newspaper and professional literature, follow special interest groups on the Internet and in social networking, participate on LinkedIn, etc., you'll find people. Being alert to opportunity becomes a way of life.

13. Determine your initial pay rate.

Look back in this book for simple formulas. Start by determining a per hour rate even if you plan to quote by-the-project fees.

Think about what numbers feel right for you. As I've written earlier, this number is not tattooed on your forehead for all eternity. But you absolutely need a number in mind for your initial calculations.

Next steps

- Test your hourly figure on yourself. Say it out loud. Do you feel comfortable saying it? Will you be happy at that rate, at least initially? If you are really brave, test your number in conversations with friends and family. If you sense that your rate is too high, get in touch with why you feel that way. Is it a lack of self-confidence or a genuine sense that it is not in sync with the market? Don't put off prospecting till you have the perfect figure. This debate within your mind can postpone action forever, leaving you in analysis paralysis to the extreme.

- Rethinking your pay rate will go on forever. Ideally you'll keep raising it.

14. Inform your family, friends, colleagues, email lists, and already-established online social networks about your new business.

My method of starting a solopro freelancing or consulting business does not depend on social networking (e.g., Facebook, LinkedIn, Twitter) to get started. However, if you already have accounts in place, inform your network.

Be careful here—these services can be addictive and steal your time from more valuable marketing activities.

But if you already have a presence in place, take a few minutes to keep everyone up-to-date and stir up some good luck.

Next steps

- For now, try to update your network about the types of work you are looking for and your triumphs (!) about once a week. However, this is not top priority.

15. Join an online forum that offers quick feedback from your peers.

This is the final item on the list because it is the least important activity on Day One.

Forums and membership groups are a terrific place to get help when you need it. Sometimes you'll ask for ideas on how to handle a problem client or how to implement a technical aspect of a project. Also, watch for general information that is always of interest, like sample contracts.

Such forums may be available through:

- Professional membership associations
- Yahoo or Google groups
- LinkedIn, Facebook, and other social networking outlets
- Fee-based membership and Mastermind groups organized by experts
- Authors in your subject area

You have to give in order to get. So get involved and stay involved even when you don't have an immediate need.

On the other hand, let your conscience be your guide. Don't let gabbing online distract you from work and marketing responsibilities.

Remember always that what you are posting online is visible to untold numbers of people. Don't post anything that detracts from your professional reputation and relationships. No-no's include any statements that your clients or their businesses are boring or out of touch, revelations that you are going to the pool even though you've promised a client immediate turnaround, or anything negative about client creativity, decisiveness, cooperation, etc. Even if you give readers no hints about the client's identity, the client may recognize himself.

Next steps

- It may take a while to find the right group(s). Ask others in your field for recommendations and do online research.

- Use your email signature (or key parts of it) in forum posts so that potential clients can contact you on the spot if so moved.

- And of course, in the future stay active in your forum and keep growing professionally.

That's it for Day One!

Congratulations! Your solopro practice is a reality. You have all the pieces in place to start contacting prospects tomorrow and begin generating real income.

The beautiful thing is that it's so easy to improve upon each of the fifteen steps in this electronic age. When you have a great marketing idea, hear some terrific business advice, or decide on some refinement, you can easily implement it when you have some spare time.

Continuing your marketing efforts will be intrinsic to your business throughout its life. Many self-employed people come to enjoy the marketing—both strategizing and implementing—as much or more than the work itself.

Tomorrow

On Day Two, the most important action to move your solo-pro business forward is to make phone calls. If this is difficult for you, commit to only a single call. Then try a few more.

You can control what you do, but you cannot control the response of others. In other words, you can determine how many calls you will make but not how many assignments you will receive.

So set an action goal: Fifty calls a day *is* ambitious but it may be do-able and you *are* fired up with ambition right now, no? This doesn't mean you will talk to fifty people. Often you will merely leave a message. Count each time you give your message, whether someone is on the other end of the line or not. Don't count disconnected phone numbers, brief interchanges with the receptionist, or other calls where you don't tell your message.

Since you will be tying up your phone, check back for voicemail messages frequently and give top priority to returning calls from prospects immediately. (I detest the beeping when call waiting disrupts my phone conversations. Depending on the technology, I key in a code to my phone so that I am not interrupted during my outgoing calls. Because I check voicemail often, I can still respond to calls quickly.)

After you make your day's calls, task number two is to identify *more* people to call. At the pace I recommend, you'll go through names rapidly.

After you have completed your calls for the day, congratulate yourself for a full day of work. Reward yourself with a coffee break, trip outdoors, single TV program (but don't let it consume the rest of your day), or whatever works for you.

Once your daily phone calls are done, the following are some additional marketing activities I'd advise dipping into as appropriate for you.

1. Determine and implement any marketing projects especially relevant to your specialty.

I've listed fifteen things to do when you first start your solo-pro freelance or consulting practice. This is a general list that can apply to most any type of work.

Something else may be really important if it relates clearly to the kind of work you do. If you design websites, you need to get your own website up quickly. If you already have one but it is totally irrelevant (e.g., fun and games when you will be offering corporate–type services), your new site may require significant—and prompt—effort.

The same goes for writing, photography, and many other types of services. You know best what potential clients expect to see from you!

2. Gather portfolio pieces, work samples, worksheets, references, etc.

Pull together what you have on hand to demonstrate your expertise. Depending on your work, PDFs may be the way to go. You can post them on your website (if you have one) or send them via email upon request.

Avoid using postal mail to convey materials. It's slow and unreliable, and going to the post office can be really inconvenient. Plus it's expensive—both for printing the materials and for postage—and outdated.

Overnight delivery services are faster and they convey importance to what you are sending. However, this option is also substantially more costly.

LinkedIn is the perfect place for many of the examples of your work and expertise. Explore its possibilities, such as for posting portfolio samples and PowerPoint presentations. While these options may not contribute to attaining a 100%

score for a totally completed profile, they may still be worth the effort.

3. Create a website.

An effective website is a great asset to your solopro practice. But then, so is a blog. And then there are sites that function like websites but use blog technology. And there are social networking sites, such as Facebook business pages, that can also substitute for a website.

The big question is what purpose will the website/blog/fan page/whatever serve? If you are not sure where you are headed with this, continue to develop your LinkedIn profile for now.

Alternatively, here are two easy ways to get started with a website or other format:

Post your résumé, adding your photo if you have a good one. Borrow some of the copy you have already created, such as the emails written to follow up on your phone calls, for headline copy.

Then tweak your résumé as you wish. You are free to ignore any conventions of résumé writing. You don't need to list all dates of employment, think up stories to explain employment gaps, or include jobs that don't contribute to the service you now offer. And you certainly don't need any lame employment objective that may currently grace the top of your document!

Alternative number two: Post the "top 10 ways [your name] can help you [insert what you do]."

For each number insert a benefit of working with you. Of course, like anything else electronic, this list isn't engraved in stone. Feel free to improve the list over time.

Prefer benefits to features. Features describe you or your services, while benefits relate these features to your prospect.

In other words, benefits are more sales-y and appealing.

For instance, "ten years of sales-coaching experience" is a feature of the consultant. "Help sales force increase sales by 25% by teaching proven conversion techniques" may be the resulting benefit. In another example, "implementation of project management principles" may be the feature; "reduce duration of projects by two months or more" could be the associated benefit.

You may be thinking of counting down from ten to one, like David Letterman's lists. It works for Dave because he is going for humor. The tenth item is likely to be as funny as the first. But if you are going for serious, start with the most important reason because it will be sure to show up on the reader's screen without any scrolling down.

Whatever you do, do not post *under construction* on your website. That's a given and a relic. Websites are always being worked on. Simple contact info, as found on your business card, will suffice when you haven't had a chance to post anything else.

To the point:

• Get your business up and running in a single day with fifteen distinct action steps.

• Keep it simple. Don't sweat the small decisions and don't attempt perfection. You can revisit any of these action steps at any time.

• You will continue to develop these marketing elements and add others to the mix throughout the life of your business.

Step 8

Stand Still! Postpone These Marketing Techniques Until Later . . . or Until Never

If you've done any online research, read books, or simply brainstormed your own marketing ideas, you are probably overwhelmed with things you *could* do. Some of these may be appropriate down the road, but most are not good at the outset.

Step 8 is about standing still. I'll describe some of the exciting marketing activities that may be beckoning for your attention . . . and why you should postpone them.

The experts recommend many of these ideas as easy and fast ways to develop a clientele. However, *easy* is in the eyes of the person doing them, and these activities, performed expertly in a way that does not humiliate you before large numbers of people, are not so easy. That doesn't mean they are too difficult to do, but simply that you are being misled if you think you can whip these items off in a few minutes or even hours if you have never done them before.

As for *fast*, most marketing activities, for maximum effectiveness, require repeated contacts with the customer, perhaps five times or more. Most of the activities below get their power from developing a *relationship* with the prospect. That can't be done in a brief period of time, almost by definition.

Just because the people selling services and coaching on the Internet say that their pet activity is easy and fast, does not mean that it is a modern-day miracle. Successful marketing of any type takes time and sustained effort.

(That's true of telephoning too. However, it is often the best way to develop an initial clientele over a limited span of calendar time.)

So here we go with what not to do, at least for now:

1. Don't write a business plan.

Business plans sound wonderful, but unless you are going out for a loan or venture capital, you'll never need one.

Sure, all the books about starting a business start with *the plan*. Theoretically, it makes sense. Start at the beginning. A calendar of planning does sound smart, but it is almost unworkable for a new business.

Here's the first catch: creating a plan doesn't automatically give you the ideas that make it real. If you sit down to write your plan first thing, you may find yourself staring at a blank computer screen, with your brain equally blank.

Ideas come about through action. As you start to discuss your work with prospects (called *telephoning*) and actually carry out assignments, solid business ideas will come to you as you drive, shower, shave, and read guru emails.

Then there is the issue of available time. If you don't have the time to start a blog today, why would you plan to establish one next November when you ideally are busy with work from paying clients?

Savor your ideas, of course. As you have ideas for new services to offer or future marketing projects, note them in a file folder in your drawer or make an electronic record. Clip, print, or otherwise save useful advice you come across so you will have it when you are ready to move forward on a new idea.

2. Don't conduct market research.

If you already have confidants in your marketplace, certainly ask for their feedback. That's a valid type of marketing research.

However, you may also be thinking of phoning or visiting potential clients solely to *assess their needs* or *measure the market*. If you are going to contact strangers, why not just ask for their business? In other words, contacting prospects is a form of marketing research too, and the advantage is that it just may drum up assignments.

Sometimes as you phone you will chance upon a contact who is chatty. Perhaps they have freelanced or consulted or maybe they respond to a "warm" connection you have made in your call, such as a mutual acquaintance or membership in a professional association. Don't pass up an opportunity to discuss the market. Ask if they use services such as yours. Ask if they are approached by many other consultants or freelancers. Ask if there are any specific services they particularly desire.

A far-reaching marketing research program is just doubling your effort. First you'll call everyone to research. Then you'll call the same people to offer your services. Another problem is that some people probably say they are *researching* when they are actually hoping the person on the other end of the line will offer them work. This is disingenuous to say the least, if not quite a lie. You're still left facing the inevitable: making the phone call to ask for work.

Marketing research was developed to save money by preventing untested yet expensive marketing campaigns, such as those for consumer products, which cost in the millions and include extensive TV advertising. Starting a one-person solo-pro practice costs almost nothing except time, so consolidate the marketing process by going right for clients, with research as an add-on when convenient.

3. Don't research prospects at length.

Undoubtedly, every call will not receive due consideration from the person phoned. So why research a company at length to isolate some specific pain they need eased? A prospect merits substantial attention, I've concluded, only if they request one-on-one communications with you.

You may fear that at the first phone call a prospect will ask you a question you can't answer. If that happens, simply tell them that if they are interested in exploring XYZ opportunity in depth, you will prepare more fully to talk to them at a time you can schedule right now. Ask them to send you any relevant information and you will read their website and other information to prepare for a phone or office meeting, as appropriate. Nothing wrong with the truth. Your time is valuable and you only invest time in intensive analysis when the occasion calls for it.

Recognizing that your call may not be answered and you may only have the opportunity to leave a voicemail message, you don't have to research sales data for the past four quarters or their international marketing plans just in case they pick up their phone.

4. Don't find specific problems and propose that you solve them.

This comes up frequently in communications fields. If you find a website rife with grammatical errors, should you go ahead and correct the errors unasked and send them on to the owner, suggesting your proofreading services? If the website is poorly designed, should you show them how you would fix it?

Sometimes this works, but a lot of times it doesn't. Here's why: people who care enough about typos and designs to fix them would not have a site that is truly appalling. Furthermore, people are sensitive and don't like to work with those who point out that they are incompetent (or that they approve the work of those who are incompetent). And finally, each of these prospects takes too much time unless you have a special reason for believing you can get their attention.

If you insist on critiquing, start with compliments along the lines of, "I saw your website and was impressed with the breadth of your product line and your strong marketing message. I think you may be the perfect candidate for my web services because you are ready to go to the next level. I developed Competitor XYZ's site and I think we can make your website a real sales machine as well."

Can't think of anything positive yet important to say about the website? Next! They won't spend real money, and even if you can sign them up for your services, you'll go crazy trying to attain standards beyond their comprehension.

5. Don't obsess over how to introduce yourself in networking situations.

Quick, tell me what you do.

This request may be your biggest nightmare because you know you should answer in a way that is well stated and brief and appealing and earnest and conversation provoking and perfectly delivered with both precision and warmth. No stammering allowed.

So you work on what to say, but meanwhile you have to get

out there and say something so you flounder and fake it and worry about it. I've even heard people apologize. They explain themselves perfectly adequately but they've been taught that their intro or elevator speech or whatever they call it should be as momentous as an Oscar acceptance speech.

First off, you don't need this tremendous prepared statement from day one. Just like you don't need a website or a professionally designed logo or a blog with a year of entries on the day you open your virtual doors. It's perfectly reasonable to state simply what you do. Time, thought, and practice will polish your words like a stone in one of those polishing gizmos.

Meanwhile, don't get all fancy-schmancy.

There are all sorts of names, formats, and prescribed time lengths for these intros depending on the guru teaching them and the circumstances in which they will be delivered. When introducing yourself, whether to a single individual or in front of a large meeting, it's better to say too little than too much. I can think of nothing more annoying than people who wear out their welcome by monopolizing more than their fair share of the time available with success stories and testimonials they have received.

Regardless of the specifics of the situation, I recommend going for clarity. People with spending authority, especially in large companies, want to understand specifically what you do. Then they can determine the benefits and if your service relieves their *pain*. Watch out for vague words, dual meanings, and imprecise descriptions that may confuse, not increase, understanding. A *communications consultant* could mean you help executives write speeches or that you advise homeowners on how many cable boxes they need. A *marketing person* may be selling used cars or studying the demographics of the Chinese beer market. Watch out too for such generic and shifty words as *systems*, *processes*, and *planning*.

Remember earlier in this book when I wrote about a writer friend who identified himself as "writer" on his business cards? It also works when you stand up to introduce yourself to a group, though honestly, you're not overstaying your welcome to expand your remarks beyond a single word.

6. Don't attend networking meetings.

Frankly, I'm hesitant to recommend most people I've met through networking. I know nothing about their work. And just as frankly, how can they refer me to others simply because my blouse coordinates with my pants and I have business cards on hand?

It takes months, if not years, of acquaintance to be sufficiently knowledgeable to properly recommend someone to others. Throw in standard networking tools, like rehearsed elevator speeches and abrasive self-confidence morphing into pushiness, and I find myself not feeling any warmth towards many of the people I meet at these things. I am not familiar with the quality of their work, and I am not eager to work with them. If I won't refer them to others, I certainly don't expect them to do it for me.

In enumerating the reasons I dislike networking, that's just for starters. Here are some more negatives.

Call me contrarian, but I think most networking activities are yucky. You might not expect to see this from someone who can comfortably telephone, but there it is. I can't help think that others are turned off by much of what is called networking, but it seems to be so essential that they can't face up to their dislike of it.

If you have found an organization whose meetings and members you enjoy, go ahead and count it as pleasure. If you find the programs educational and they develop your knowledge and skills, those are reasons enough to attend. But if you think you'll get clients quickly, don't get your hopes up. Even those who excel at networking report that it takes months to develop relationships.

Perhaps you think telephoning is too scary and that maybe networking will be easier. But that's not my experience. Networking is a highly nuanced form of interaction that takes way more social skills than telephoning. And when you run out of things to say, instead of just saying *thank you* and hanging up, you have to invent a polite way to extricate yourself.

Networking advocates remind us that our interactions must be mutually beneficial. This means you must spend as much time listening to others and helping them solve their problems as they spend on you. You must note the phone numbers, articles, and other aids you promise them and follow up promptly when you return to your desk. So right off the bat, half of your activity is about helping them, not yourself. Sure, it may be reciprocated someday, but probably not in time to pay next month's rent.

Networking can be hugely expensive. In large cities, you may spend over $20 to park and $35 or more for a chicken breast and broccoli. The event itself can eat up hours of time, and in urban areas travel may claim additional hours on the road or by train.

Distance of upcoming conferences is an important criterion for determining which organizations to join. Remember that joining an organization is not a lifelong decision; membership only lasts a year. So if the National Association of Widget Designers meets next month in your hometown and the Widget Designers Society meets 3,000 miles away six months from now, that's a major consideration in determining which to join. If you don't become an officer, there's no reason you can't join one this year and try the other next year.

Speaking of being an officer, temper your enthusiasm for

volunteering. Life is not fair and there's no guarantee that fellow members will give you dibs on assignments in recognition for all your hard work. In fact, it may work exactly the opposite. Someone who attends the meeting but does no organizational work may be hitting up someone at your table for an assignment while you're off reminding the kitchen that five attendees ordered the vegetarian entrée and another is allergic to shellfish.

The more niche-y the gathering, the more expensive and the bigger distance to travel. Out in the suburbs and rural areas, you can find chambers of commerce, Rotary chapters, and similar multi-industry events. These may be low cost, but the people you will meet typically represent the broadest range of business activities, both service and product-oriented. Niche gatherings are usually held in the largest metropolitan areas with the highest meeting costs, both in registration fees and travel expenses. And the tightest niches have only national conferences, requiring you to travel from your home in New England to Vancouver if you want to make it to this year's big event.

Looking ahead, as you narrow your niche, many of your initial organizations will fall by the wayside. Too few participants will work in your niche and you'll reach the point where it's not worth your time to attend. Then all your effort to date is irrelevant as you switch to more attractive organizations and their events.

In fact, the most relevant association may only meet on an international basis. This may be a very expensive organization in which to become involved, where most members have their ways paid by large corporations. You may wish to start earning money before you start spending money so aggressively.

All this leads to the most important question you can ask about an organization: Why join at all?

- To gain access to the membership directory. A good membership directory has complete contact information, including telephone numbers and email addresses. Such a directory is the gold standard of prospecting lists.

- Membership in itself is a claim that can warm up your phone approach. Whether introducing yourself on a call or leaving a voicemail message, remind the person you are calling that, "I am a fellow member of XYZ association."

- Membership in a narrowly focused organization demonstrates that you are serious about your niche and you are an industry insider.

- Membership perks may include access to a password-protected, informative website and other specialized resources. Now that you no longer have coworkers in neighboring cubicles to bounce ideas off, professional organizations can help fill the information and professional camaraderie gaps.

7. Don't hire a telemarketer to make phone calls for you.

Most telemarketers stink. They drone through a script they didn't write and don't understand. It's so easy to hang up on them.

Furthermore, they can't sign the prospect up. You, the pro, will still need to follow up, discuss the assignment, negotiate terms, finalize the arrangement, etc. Sorry, you're going to have to get on the phone, like it or not.

Third, telemarketers can't develop rapport as you can. Once they say they are calling for someone else, they may not develop any type of relationship, garner any information about the services the company does use, or anything else.

Telemarketers face all the marketing problems you face

with one more: they are not you. They don't know your service as well as you do, they cannot advise on your specialty, and they can't finalize anything. They don't have your credibility.

8. Don't do newsletters and blogs.

It's easy to start out with the ambition to blog daily or at least three times a week. That's because you have so much free time at the moment. But will you enjoy doing this work for free when you have enough paying work to fill your days and haunt your weekends?

Newsletters, blogs, and other recurring communications demand a long-term commitment. In fact, the whole point is to develop a relationship with the reader so they know, like, and trust you before calling you to discuss an assignment. These activities can be sl-o-o-o-w to develop clients. It takes multiple issues to make much of an impression. And you still have to figure out how your readers will make the leap from enjoying your free advice to paying you for it.

If your marketing efforts work, you'll soon be too busy to carry on this vehicle week after week (or even every month). It makes a worse impression to start and stop repeatedly than never to start at all.

Furthermore, do you have enough fresh ideas to keep writing on schedule? Are you a good and fast writer? Do you like to write?

Do you have the genesis of a readership? Newsletters and blogs are pointless unless you will put forth effort to build your readership. There's no point developing something to send out if you have no one to send it to. (Though on the other hand, one or two good names are more valuable than thousands of irrelevant email addresses. You are under no obligation to reveal how many names are receiving your newsletter or blog.)

One more potential challenge: It may be especially difficult to generate content when you are just starting your practice and not benefiting from the personal interactions or engaging projects that spark writing ideas and success stories worthy of boasting.

9. Don't issue print brochures.

Your website is your brochure. You may never need a print version. Or you may want to present key information in a handy PDF format that is certain to print off exactly as you intend it to look.

Avoid mailing out anything, at least at the beginning. The best prospects are computer literate and can print out anything they need on their own. Those who want paper mailings are either on an ego trip ("I'm too important to bother with printing; if you want my business you'll cater to me with paper mailings.") or they are behind the times and not comfortable with the computer.

The exception would be if you are exhibiting at a conference or meeting with prospects in person. In this case, it may be useful to have something in print. If this is the case, print the minimum number of copies needed.

10. Don't do public speaking.

There can be weeks or even months of lag time between soliciting engagements and actually speaking. Then there can be additional time between speaking and getting paying work. Just as with newsletters and blogs, it may take months to see tangible results, i.e., money, from these activities.

If you are going to do speaking, be sure your audience is the right audience for you. Just because you can line up unpaid engagements at community luncheons doesn't mean it's worth the effort.

If you think speaking will be easier than telephoning, think again. I've read a zillion articles and emails that the only thing people fear more than death itself is public speaking. (This "fact" is attributed to Jerry Seinfeld and its accuracy is questionable.) I've never seen a survey that ranked *talking on the telephone* in second place. Or even in the top ten or twenty...

Don't speak publicly unless you are prepared to spend enough time to prepare yourself with carefully thought-out content, attractive handouts, a classy PowerPoint if appropriate to your topic, and lots of practice!

The worst speakers prepare minimal content and then ask for questions, pretending that they want to talk about what really interests the audience rather than droning on about what interests them personally. But an audience of even moderate sophistication can detect indifference. Who would entrust a project to a speaker who is passive, short on compelling messages, and simply lazy?

In the future after your solopro practice is off the ground, public speaking may prove an effective marketing effort. However, I'm telling you how to start getting paying assignments in thirty days, and like many of the other marketing techniques in this chapter, public speaking is seldom fast enough.

11. Don't pay for print advertising.

The best thing that can be said for paid advertising is that you can write it off your taxes. I've never heard of it working for solopros.

Darn expensive and even the experts say it takes multiple exposures to be effective.

Some advertising is placed in fundraising programs, high school yearbooks, etc. It's not so expensive and what you are doing is donating to charity. If this is your intent, go ahead. But don't hold your breath waiting for business.

12. Don't advertise in phone directories.

I haven't tried it myself and I haven't heard many success stories. Its greatest likelihood for success is for specialties that must be delivered in person where both parties know that nothing is going to happen without geographic proximity. I'd guess it works for plumbers and air conditioning repairers.

There are problems in advertising freelance and consulting services in phone directories. First, some of your callers may be especially naïve and even outright crazy. People who advertise writing services, for instance, have their stories about people who want someone to write their life story for them. No money up front, of course. Isn't it enough that they're sharing their exciting story with you? You'll get paid after they're on national TV and sell a million books.

Phonebook advertising can be expensive. If you advertise in multiple directories in a hopeless attempt to cover more of your service area, it's even more costly.

There's lag time. These volumes are printed once a year on the publishers' schedules, not yours. (I'm assuming you get into the online version as soon as you pay for the year, but I've never researched this.)

Finally, most of the listings are totally useless. Take a look at "marketing consultants," for instance. What does that mean? Selling? Telemarketers? Copywriters? People who sell pens imprinted for your business? If people can't identify what you do—again, it's that clarity thing—do you think they are going to call the entire list looking for exactly your services?

13. Don't do faxing campaigns.

Spam of the worst type—in other words, totally out of date.

I used to own a fax machine. It was handy for sending out scrawled, hand-written notes or hasty sketches. Also, it was good for transmitting signatures. Now, like many other people, I create a scan and email it.

Faxing is a spammy, chicken-shit way to sneak your information out to people while avoiding in-person connection.

14. Don't send email to info@company.com.

I was talking to Bill Gates the other day about email that came in at info@microsoft.com back when he was onsite. He tells me he spent hours figuring out the exact person who should receive it. This required so much time that he found it hard to get out and play bridge with Warren Buffett.

The only instance in which *info@* email may get an interested audience is for single-person businesses where the decision maker is personally sorting out this stuff. Use personal email addresses instead!

15. Don't publish information products.

First, a disclaimer: what you are reading here is an information product.

If you've started to study marketing online, by now you've probably read that you should create and sell information products, which are more optimistically called your *information empire*. These products establish you as the authority—you *wrote the book*—and enable you to sell something (the product) to people who cannot afford your hourly rate.

Optimists say, "Make money while you sleep!" referencing twenty-four-hour e-commerce.

Maybe creating information products is the best route for you, but it's a different kind of industry. If this is what you want to do first thing, then turn your focus to this industry, not to freelancing or consulting. Publishing is a challenging field of its own so redirect yourself to learning its own requirements.

Furthermore, do you even have a subject that you are ready to prepare information products on? It's easier to begin distilling the important lessons of your field as you carry out a range of freelancing and consulting assignments for a variety of clients and then write later.

16. Don't let blogging, Facebook, LinkedIn, Twitter, etc. interfere with real marketing efforts.

Be very cautious here. Are you participating to achieve a genuine marketing objective or to postpone real work?

Online discussions can be as addictive as chocolate, as stimulating as caffeine, and infinitely interesting. But they frequently lead nowhere (and they don't pay anything).

Never let these activities substitute for telephoning if you are truly in business-generation mode! Don't let yourself off the hook for real marketing because you've been skimming LinkedIn profiles and piping in on topics 140 characters at a time.

There may be exceptions if other participants and readers are your potential clients. However, if you are looking for corporate clients, the right prospects may be difficult to identify online. Many of the people I encounter online appear to be self-employed or unemployed without access to larger corporate budgets.

Your postings must be intelligent and valuable. "Me too" or "I agree" gets your name out there but portrays you as hugely egotistical. Who cares if you simply agree?

I grant some exemptions. Elsewhere I have advised finding online professional groups that can advise you on work challenges as they arise. If you find a valuable group, reciprocate by helping others generously and participating in discussions.

17. Don't perfect your legal contract.

If you are even moderately sophisticated in the ways of business, you understand the serious threat of being sued.

The best solution to this threat is to do nothing. Don't start a solopro practice or any type of business. Offer no services. Voilà! No legal problems.

If you're looking for an excuse to avoid launching your solopro practice, here's the perfect one. The best way to avoid billions in potential fines and years in jail is to do nothing. But of course, you'll never make any money.

The second best solution is to call your attorney. The experts tell you to "call your attorney" for everything. (You *do* have an attorney who specializes in business law standing by, don't you?) Sure, pay him $750 to review your contract for a $500 assignment.

In practice, most solopros try their hand at drafting a contract early in the game as they try to answer the classic question of which comes first, the chicken or the egg? Specifically, if you are looking for your first freelance or consulting assignment, do you need a carefully crafted contract ready to go before you reach out to your first prospect?

It's rare to see an expert who explicitly recommends having the perfect contract template on your computer all ready to fill in the blanks and send it out on the spot.

However, there are experts who instill such fear that you

assume you need that contract. Otherwise, when you are offered an assignment that must be turned around in a reasonable timeframe, you won't be able to get that essential contract signed and filed before you start the work, putting you out of the running right from the start.

Anyone who reads the news, whether online or hardcopy, knows that modern society is litigious; people love to sue. Oh no, we think. At the first mistake, no matter how well intentioned we are, clients will sue us, just like the coffee lady who sued McDonald's.

It's easy to panic but hold on a minute. McDonald's has much deeper pockets than any of us. An attorney is more open to taking a contingency case against McDonald's than against us.

There probably is not much litigation against individual freelancers or consultants. Here's an unscientific experiment I conducted a few years ago. Back when I was on the board of a local freelancers' organization, we were waiting for a final member to show up so we could start our business meeting. I filled the empty time by asking if anyone present had ever been sued. The count was zero (among perhaps seven people).

In practice, writing an all-purpose, all-inclusive contract on day one is way premature. At this point you are employed because you are doing marketing work every day, but in another sense, it doesn't count until money's coming in as well. Always avoid spending money, on contracts, insurance, whatever, until you're making money.

If you want to start getting work quickly, you have to start prospecting quickly. This means putting preparatory work—including contract development—on a back burner.

Back burner doesn't mean taking it off the stove entirely. Start a file, either by taking a manila folder, labeling it, and placing it in your file drawer or by creating an electronic file.

Then add to the file over time by researching your industry for sample contracts. This includes asking colleagues, asking officers or administrators of professional organizations to which you belong, searching through books relevant to your practice, asking on Yahoo, LinkedIn, and Facebook groups, Google searches, etc.

Ask yourself what exposures worry you most. Consider adding text that gets you off the hook for things you don't want to be responsible for, such as printing expenses if something written is later found to have an error and needs to be redone. For instance, when I write résumés, I alert the client that she—not me—has final responsibility for proofreading and any other quality issues. Some freelancers and consultants send one-way emails or print letters of understanding rather than pursue full-blown signed contracts for small assignments.

As we get started, we are prone to think that the perfect contract prevents all problems. Not true. The integrity of the client is far more important than the contract . . . by far!

If you prospect among large clients, they will probably offer their own contract. You will either accept the contract or propose revisions to their contract. If all your clients are large, you may never have occasion to offer your own contract.

Structure the agreement so you get paid a significant percentage of the fee—or even the full amount—before you start. The very worst that can happen is that you miss out on the final payment rather than the full amount.

The speed with which a client sends the first check says more about the client than any contract ever could. I've had clients overnight me a check for 10:30 A.M. arrival so I would start their project immediately. When people want you, it's amazing how fast the bureaucracy can get things done.

Walk away (maybe). If your gut is telling you that a leakproof contract is essential with this client, it's better to turn down the assignment than to work till 2 A.M. crafting the perfect agreement. There are far worse things than not having paying work. For instance, devoting lots of time to an assignment and then not getting paid for it.

By the way, to this day I do not require a contract that is signed by the client. I email a simple proposal to the client that describes the project briefly and clarifies amounts due and when they are due. In my case, as a writer, I may clarify that I only provide copy in Microsoft Word; I do no design nor do I select photos or other visual material. I may state that I am not liable for typos or other errors, but since my work is corporate and is reviewed by many internal staffers, I often skip this. I do not require this email to be signed and returned to me—just remit the initial payment, please.

Note: The legal organization of your enterprise, e.g., corporation, LLC, sole proprietorship, etc., also has liability implications. This topic is beyond the scope of this publication. Consult an attorney for further information.

Disclaimer: I'm not an attorney (obviously!). For legal advice, consult an attorney.

To the point:

- Create time to contact prospects directly by taking off your plate everything you can postpone. I've proposed seventeen widely recommended action steps to skip, at least as you start out.

- Bask in the luxurious sensation of chores being lifted from your shoulders. Aaaahhh...

Congratulations!

Now you know how to land the ideal business clients for your freelance and consulting services. This process works. I've re-launched my writing and research practice several times after periods of full-time employment, and I've always attracted assignments within weeks.

Phoning the best prospects to offer professional services you have mastered in corporate employment is the most direct route to self-employment success. It may take weeks, but the process is effective. Making it work for you requires patience and conscientious action. It's easy to get discouraged and quit after a few calls, and you may see little happening in the way of positive results at first.

Remember that if it were easy, everyone would do it. And if everyone did it, it wouldn't work as well. Keep at it and you will enjoy the payoff.

Begin now. Professional fulfillment and success await you.

Appendix 1

Sample Prospecting Email

This is typical of the emails that I send in follow-up to phone conversations. It has evolved over years of marketing.

Obviously, it is not ready for your use. You'll need to customize it so much that you might as well start from scratch.

Dear [insert first name]:

Here is the information about my services in insurance writing and research that we discussed a few moments ago. My website, www.dianawrites.com, supplements the following.

In addition, I've written a special report I'd like to share with you on Thought-Leader Writing. Please request it from my website. You'll also receive my occasional newsletter so we can keep in touch. (You can easily unsubscribe at any time.)

And let's connect on LinkedIn. (I'm sending you an invite today.)

Please let me know if I can provide further information. I hope we can work together soon.

Diana Schneidman
630.XXX.XXXX (Chicago area)

Writing and research to inform and inspire

insurance ~ financial ~ business

You may well have read my writing . . . but you didn't know I wrote it. Over the years I've written for leading industry executives, Fortune 100 companies, and international trade and training organizations. I've also been published in trades and general-circulation newspapers under my own byline (formerly Diana Cohen Harris).

I would like to help you, as an industry executive, deliver effective written communications and presentations while restricting the time you must personally devote to such projects.

I work with executives and managers at leading insurance and financial companies to develop outstanding communications, often within tight timeframes. My lead strength is integrating the right information with effective writing (though I've successfully done almost every type of corporate writing there is).

My writing and research skills are top-notch, and the depth of my dedication to your project makes my work truly outstanding. I am creative in project conceptualization, yet proudly fanatic about detail. When I commit to your deadline, I move heaven and earth to meet it. As time gets tight, I will provide cell-phone access and adapt to international time zones to get the job done right. **So tell me your concerns about the finer points and I'll follow through. I really care.**

Expertise that benefits your project

- Consulting and staff experience in marketing research, marketing communications, and competitive intelligence in insurance, asset management, and business

- CLU (Chartered Life Underwriter), CPCU (Chartered

Property/Casualty Underwriter), and CMFC (Chartered Mutual Funds Counselor) designations

- Master's degree in library science, with strong skills in print and electronic research

- Additional coursework and experience in knowledge management

- Diverse writing experience:

    o Corporate documents (that nail the voice of your organization's culture)

    o Speeches and PowerPoint slides

    o Newspapers, trade magazines, and scholarly journals: news articles and features

    o Marketing research reports

    o Marketing communications

    o Direct mail

    o Web content and emails

    o Advertising

    o Training

    o Correspondence

    o Professional career writing, including résumés

- Insight and ingenuity in developing provocative themes and persuasive messages from numbers and facts

- Perceptivity and accuracy in organizing and analyzing data

- Strengths in conducting all types of interviews: staff input, journalistic, and competitive intelligence

- Skills in working with legal and regulatory restrictions in the mutual fund industry

Let's get started.

Let's discuss your writing and research needs. I can provide writing samples appropriate to your plans.

Simply phone me at **630.xxx.xxxx** (Chicago area) so we can proceed.

I hope we can work together soon!

—Diana

Appendix 2

Cash In on Your Skills: How to Turn Your Work Experience into a Highly Profitable, Home-Based Virtual Assistant Business

By Kathy Goughenour

Working as a VA since 2000, Kathy has earned as much as $106,000 annually while working from home, usually in her pajamas. In 2008, Kathy launched her Expert VA Training program. As a working Virtual Assistant—and Founder, Trainer, and Coach of Expert VA Training—Kathy advises VAs how to get more clients, achieve their income goals, and build the business of their dreams. Learn more at www.expertVAtraining.com.

A relatively new career stands out as a reliable earning option whether the economy is up or down: being a Virtual Assistant (or VA).

What is a Virtual Assistant?

A Virtual Assistant provides services to clients who may live around the corner or halfway around the world.

A career as a Virtual Assistant could be perfect for a laid-off middle manager, a retiree who needs extra cash, or a mom who wants to work from home. Since just about any office task can be performed remotely except bringing someone coffee, filing papers in manila folders, or greeting people coming into the office, the field has a surprisingly large scope.

VAs work in a wide variety of roles: executive assistants, e-commerce specialists, author assistants, ghostwriters, data entry personnel, and much more.

As a Virtual Assistant, you work from your home using your computer and your phone to communicate with your clients. You offer administrative, technical, and/or support services to clients who are typically small business owners, solopreneurs, or entrepreneurs.

What services do Virtual Assistants provide?

Here's a checklist of just a few of the services today's Virtual Assistants provide:

- Write and/or set up monthly newsletters

- Set up and maintain online shopping carts

- Edit video and audio files

- Write, edit, and proofread

- Draft letters and reports and prepare correspondence

- Prepare PowerPoint presentations

- Maintain client information databases

- Write and email follow-up letters to clients, including managing email marketing systems such as Aweber and Constant Contact

- Perform bookkeeping and accounting duties

- Manage affiliate programs
- Market products and services
- Update and maintain websites
- Research
- Manage a team of Virtual Assistants

How do you translate your skills into a Virtual Assistant business?

You'll want to determine not only what skills you're going to offer, which is called your niche, but also the industry you want to offer your skills to, which is called your target market.

So which comes first, the niche or the target market? It depends on you.

- If you have a set of skills that will work in a variety of markets, start with the skills you want to offer and then choose the target market.

- If you have extensive knowledge about a particular industry, start with the target market and then determine which skills you want to offer that industry.

Choosing your target market

When choosing your target market, consider the following:

- What types of small businesses or industries are you already an expert in or do you have experience with?

- Is the industry familiar with VAs? If not, you'll have to spend time and effort educating them about this. If you need to make money ASAP, you may want to find an industry that is familiar with VAs.

- Does the typical small business owner or entrepreneur in

this industry have the ability and desire to pay for a VA's services?

- Does this industry have a built-in need for ongoing support year-round?

- Is there an abundance of small businesses or entrepreneurs in this industry?

- Does the industry have a professional/trade association? If yes, that's a good sign that it is a large enough industry for you to have plenty of opportunities to get clients.

- Are there magazines and blogs that service that industry?

Do your homework and investigate any target markets you're interested in to answer all the above questions.

Checklist of small businesses that need VAs

Here's a short list of the types of small businesses you may want to consider as your target market. It is in no way all inclusive, but, hopefully, it will get your creative juices flowing and help you come up with the area in which you want to specialize.

- Internet marketers

- Coaches

- Trainers

- Consultants

- Real estate agents

- Mortgage providers

- Restaurants/caterers/B&Bs

- Authors/writers

- Professional speakers

- Online-based retail businesses
- Doctors
- Lawyers

Choosing the skills to offer

To determine if the specific skills you want to offer are in high demand, research both online and offline. Here are some questions to answer before and during your research:

- What are your areas of expertise?
- What skills do you already have that you would like to use?
- Who is willing to pay for those skills?

Spending the time to determine your niche and target market is crucial to the success of your business. Approximately 95% of all Virtual Assistants do not specialize. However, to build your business faster and earn more, stop trying to be everything to everyone.

Instead, identify your specific niche and target market and become a true expert in those fields.

Equipment needed to start a Virtual Assistant business

There are four basic things you need (which you probably already have) to start your VA business:

1. An up-to-date computer with the most recent Microsoft Office software.

2. High-speed Internet access.

3. A phone.

4. A phone plan with low-cost long-distance and, preferably, unlimited minutes.

It is also recommend that you set up a website. Without a website, you have a big CLOSED sign on your business.

Just because you have no boss looking over your shoulder doesn't mean a Virtual Assistant business is not a job. Many people fail to make money as a Virtual Assistant because they do not take their businesses seriously enough. They do not set and maintain specific office hours; they don't make time to market their businesses; and they find it difficult to concentrate on required tasks.

To keep from falling into this trap, choose a niche and target market you are passionate about. Set specific and measurable daily, weekly, and monthly goals. You may also wish to work with a coach and a mastermind group to help hold yourself accountable.

Acknowledgments

I've worked on this book for years (off and on) and I appreciate the many experts and friends who have helped me think through and experiment and live this material. Thankfully, I have so many people to acknowledge for all their help.

My husband, Wayne, my executive VP of IT, for being my constant friend and confidant.

My three children, Faye, Herschel, and Stuart, who were my undying motivation to find freelance work as a single mother, and stepchildren Jennifer, Kimberly, and Jeffrey.

Sharon Woodhouse, editor and publishing expert extraordinaire and a true source of motivation and inspiration, in bringing out the best of my thoughts and the words to communicate them.

Phyllis Ezop, friend and marketing guru, for her patience in long, meandering conversations and untiring enthusiasm for concept development and book-title analysis.

Kathy Goughenour, VA expert and appendix author, for her wisdom.

Peter Bowerman, C.J. Hayden, Tama Kieves, Judy Murdoch, Mark Schumann, Mark Silver, Andrea Stenberg, Joan Stewart, Melissa G. Wilson, and Marcia Yudkin for their expert advice, which I have valued.

Fellow writers of the Independent Writers of Chicago (IWOC) for remarkable insights into freelancing success.

My freelance/consulting clients and my loyal, commenting blog readers for all the feedback and encouragement you have provided along the way.

Index

multitasking, 18
not while on phone!, 60
networking
compared to phoning, 95
introductions, 175–176
meetings, 177–179
and pity parties, 54–55
for solopros vs. job hunters,
56–58
strategic, 57
taking out the yuck, 55–56
newsletters. *See* email newsletters
next level, taking it to the, 67
niche
defined, 29
determining one, 29–37, 42
refining one, 30–31
testing in the marketplace, 30, 42
niches, problem, 31–34
nuisance. *See* pestering/being a
nuisance
numbers, 68–69. *See also* law of large
numbers
online forums, 164–165
organizations. *See* associations
outlook, improving one's, 19
outsourcing marketing/phoning, 45,
180–181
passion
determining yours, 21–22
as moving target, 22
required (or not) for self-
employment, 3
past clients (as most important source
of work), 44, 45
payment. *See* collections, earning
money
payment milestones, 131
PayPal, 126, 130
percentage of calls successful, 94
perfection/perfectionism. *See*
beginning imperfectly *and*

marketing, no need for perfection
pestering/being a nuisance (not!), 85,
100
phone calls/phoning, 65–103. *See also*
conversation, lists, *and* prospects.
and awareness (greater) of your
existence, 25
asking questions during, 89
best time of day for, 73–74
as best way to generate work
quickly, 5, 14
comparing results of to other
marketing methods, 95, 103
as a controllable goal, 25
as easy/easier than you'd think, 6,
24, 65
for entire lives, 6
as exchange of honest
information, 82
as free/cheap, 6
frequency of, 70–73
as helping people, 24, 26–27,
65, 74–75, 93, 102, 103. *See
also* reaching out to others
lists. *See* lists
and mobility, 6
as most direct/efficient marketing
method, 24, 28, 41, 63, 67
as not aggressive selling, 24
as not a nuisance, 100
as not spam, 75, 102
not worrying about length, 60
percentage successful, 94
as person who will be performing
work, 45
prospects. *See* prospects
quantity of, 92–94
as requiring minimal preparation,
24–25
results, seeing/waiting for, 23,
95–96
scripts. *See* scripts

About the Author

Diana Schneidman was let go from several corporate jobs and each time she profited from freelance and consulting work that lifted her spirits and helped pay the bills. Today she is a successful freelance writer and market researcher specializing in the insurance and asset management industries.

She holds a B.S. in English and French education from The Ohio State University and a Master's in Library Science from Kent State University, and resides with her husband in Bolingbrook (Chicago), IL.

About Stand Up 8 Times

Diana Schneidman founded Stand Up 8 Times to help people who want to land well-paying freelance and consulting work quickly. The company offers information products and coaching dedicated to helping people who want to take control of their lives through self-employment. Stand Up 8 Times takes its name from a Japanese proverb: "Fall down seven times, stand up eight."

Bonus: Boost Your Phoning Mindset!

Sometimes I have to get in the right mood to start making calls. I accomplish this by reviewing the positive attitudes I advocate in this book.

I've given you a headstart in enjoying uplifting thoughts as you pick up the phone. Visit *http://www.StandUp8Times.com/ mindset* to access an MP3 audio file that will boost your spirits.

I have also provided a Word file that you can revise to suit your preferences. You can even record it again in your own voice!

Enjoy!

Like this book?

Please share it with your friends, review it on Amazon, and recommend that your local public or college library purchase it.

The conversation continues . . .

I am developing new ideas and books to help beginning and mid-career freelancers and consultants succeed, and I appreciate your sharing your triumphs and challenges. Please join me at:

- **Ezine newsletter:** Sign up at *http://www.StandUp8Times.com*
- **My blog:** *http://www.standup8times.com/blog/*
- **Post your question to my blog at:** *http://budurl.com/ plspost*
- **LinkedIn:** *http://www.linkedin.com/in/dianaschneidman*
- **Twitter:** *https://twitter.com/DianaSchneidman*

Made in the USA
Lexington, KY
13 June 2015